40 MOTORING HEROES

Pioneers, Inventors, Mavericks, and Game Changers

Rod Ashley

HAWKSMOOR
PUBLISHING

First published in 2025 by Hawksmoor Publishing
Woodside, Oakamoor, ST10 3AE, UK
www.hawksmoorpublishing.com
ISBN: 978-1-914066-77-1

A CIP catalogue record for this book is available from the British Library.

ABOUT THE AUTHOR

Rod Ashley is a motoring enthusiast with a particular interest in automotive and industrial history. He has written many articles for the Road Transport History Association, of which he was a Director and the Chair; has written extensively for *Good Motoring* magazine and is the Honorary Life Vice-President of his regional branch of the road safety organisation, IAM RoadSmart.

Outside of these interests, Rod has extensive professional experience in education and skills development. After teaching and researching at Swansea University, he became the Director of the Welsh Secondary Schools Association. As Managing Partner of CATS Consultancy, he worked with bodies as diverse as the European Commission, the BBC and many universities. Rod is the author of over twenty books on education, skills and career management. He is a Fellow of the Royal Society of Arts and a Fellow of the Higher Education Academy.

Rod is the author of *Wolfram Wars: Exposing The Secret Battle in Portugal*, also published by Bennion Kearny, under their Dark River imprint.

ACKNOWLEDGEMENTS

Writing is often a solitary activity but I am indebted to my wife, Moira, for proof-reading the emerging manuscript and making astute suggestions.

My publisher, James Lumsden-Cook, as with my last book, has shown a genuine interest in the material and worked swiftly and efficiently to create the finished volume.

My youngest granddaughter, Saylor Iles, has provided inspiration from New Zealand for active problem-solving and perseverance.

Any errors are mine alone.

CONTENTS

Introduction

The automotive world is full of big characters and entrepreneurs with plenty of self-confidence. Think of Giovanni Agnelli of FIAT (who allegedly argued that "*You need an odd number of people to run a motor company and three is too many* …"), of Henry Ford's passion for efficient manufacture, or the genius for lateral thinking and space-engineering of Alec Issigonis. These are well-known names, certainly among motoring enthusiasts and even in the wider public.

However, there are also engineers, entrepreneurs and motoring godparents who have made a quieter but nonetheless significant impact upon the automotive world, not necessarily because they were shy and retiring, but simply because their efforts or names did not reach a mass audience, even if their products did. Others have had a wider societal impact through their actions or principles.

This book is a collection of lesser-known motoring figures. If some of the names are well-known to you, forgive me, but they may be little-known to a wide audience. For example, Diesel is a name well-known as a fuel or engine type, but many people do not realise that it is named after its eponymous inventor Rudolf Diesel. The extraordinary life *and death* of this Renaissance Man are intriguing.

The names that follow are, in many cases, not just inventors, innovators, engineers, financiers or others at the forefront of automotive history – individuals and their teams who made a significant impact upon motoring. They also include stories of ingenuity, determination, perseverance, fighting against norms or prejudice, and even bravery, self-sacrifice and penury. Of course, possessing such qualities does not necessarily confer sainthood or even likeability. A fair few of them demonstrated unpleasant human qualities, but we acknowledge their professional achievements. Not all made fortunes out of their ideas, but their ideas added to the wealth and enjoyment of motoring.

Let's get started!

Mary Anderson: An Unsung Heroine of Winter Motoring

If asked to name manufacturers of windscreen wiper blades, most motorists would probably be hard-pushed to name many brands – perhaps recognising just Bosch or Trico. Certainly, Mary Anderson would be unheard of, but as with many inventions, the inventor or patentee is not widely known. So, how did Mary Anderson come to be associated with a device which is now a standard safety feature on most forms of road transport, trains, ships and aircraft?

Born in Greene County, Alabama, in 1866, Mary moved as a young woman to Birmingham, Alabama, in 1889 with her widowed mother and sister, the state's largest city at that time. Here she became a real estate developer, building with her family the Fairmont Apartments. In 1902, Mary made her first visit to New York City and, for someone used to the warmth of southern Alabama, she now experienced weather she had never previously seen – snow! From her city tram, she noted that the driver regularly had to dismount to clean the screen so that he could continue safely. What, she pondered, could help the driver see clearly without having to dismount? Had she not taken that trip to New York, would she have ever been inspired as an inventor?

Dedication and perseverance

On her return to Alabama, Mary started to sketch out ideas for a windscreen cleaning device. Mary's design featured a rubber blade attached to a swinging arm, with a spindle through the glass screen connecting the blade to an internal handle. Would that be possible? She set to work writing up a description, and when she was happy with it, applied for a patent. For her, a key element was that it should be a temporary, removable device which could be stowed away in fine weather and thus not mar the visual appearance of the vehicle.

Mary moved quickly. By 18 June 1903, the patent was filed, and by 10 November the same year, the US Patent Office had awarded her patent number 743,801 for the Window Cleaning Device – a patent which would endure until 1920.

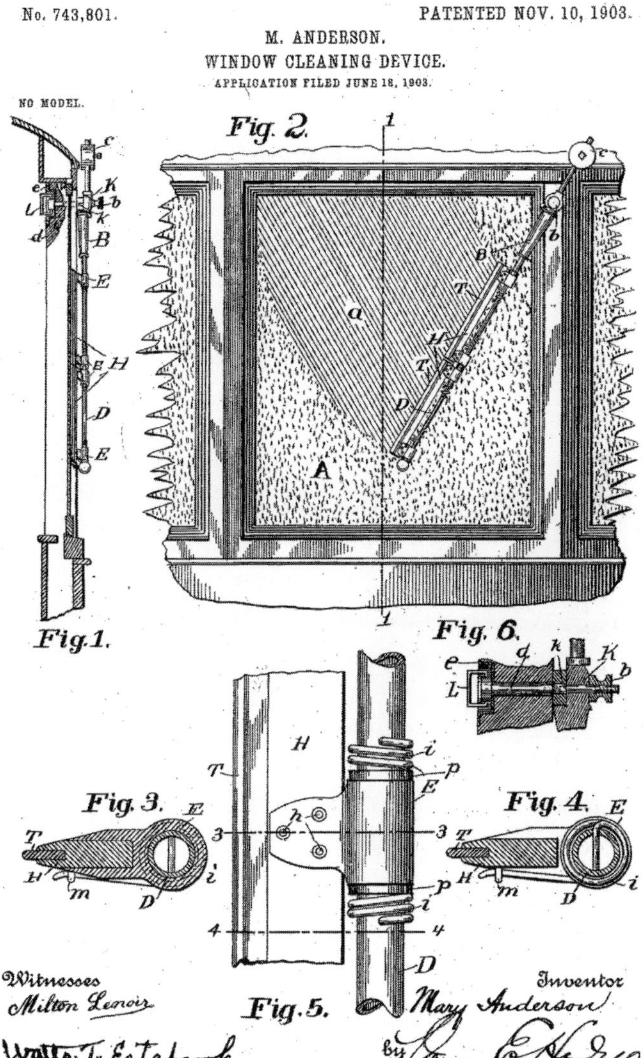

Then, of course, began the hard slog of trying to interest manufacturers in the device. Alas, no automobile manufacturer, tramcar manufacturer or component manufacturer seemed taken with the concept. After all, it didn't rain every day and some US states, particularly in the west, had minimal rainfall, so was it really necessary? Many cars were open-topped and still lacked windscreens. They were used only in fine weather. And, of course, safety equipment in vehicles of any type was to remain rudimentary for decades.

Bouncing back from rejection

The letter Mary received, dated 20 June 1906, from her patent agents (responsible for trying to license her patent to third parties), Messrs Dinning and Eckenstein, is revealing. Firstly, it reminds us that processing any patent is a lengthy affair – three years after submitting her patent, Mary is still doggedly pursuing its commercial application. Her efforts are all the more remarkable given that she is a spinster in a male-dominated world, and she has no males arguing on her behalf. Secondly, the patent agents' address is Montreal in Canada, illustrating that an agent outside the USA has examined the patent. Thirdly, the reasons cited for rejection of the patent are "We do not consider it to be of such commercial value as would warrant our undertaking its sale." Now that may have been the initial response of a manufacturer selling into the arid conditions of California, Utah or Arizona – but could not an agent based in cold, wet and snowy Montreal see the potential beyond this? Detroit, on the US side of the Great Lakes, was establishing itself as the centre for automotive manufacturers, yet was hardly noted for its balmy climate.

Mary continued her battle for her road safety invention, but to no avail. She never received any money for her invention or efforts, although she did live to see wipers fitted on cars. In 1922, just two years after Mary's patent expired, the flagship General Motors marque, Cadillac, incorporated windscreen wipers, not just as an optional extra, but as standard equipment!

Others take the credit

Far from being crushed by rejection, Mary fought on, determined to see her invention help improve motor transport. Indeed, she lived on until the middle of the 20th century, by which time windscreen wipers had become standard equipment. From the weird vacuum-controlled system on my father's Ford Anglia 100E (requiring a twirl of the vacuum dial depending on which gear you were in) to today's rain-sensitive, automatic wipers, Mary's invention is a boon to all drivers, particularly in winter conditions.

Throughout her life, Mary pursued her entrepreneurial activities until her death in 1953. She continued to manage the Fairmont apartment building she had built in Birmingham, Alabama, as well as operating a cattle ranch and vineyard in Fresno, California. In 2011, over a century after registering her patent, Mary received the great accolade of being inducted into the US National Inventors Hall of Fame. Whether to cope with light showers, torrential downpours or falling snow (but never to shift heavy accumulations of snow on the screen), her device's development and the tale of her determination and 'bouncebackability' is an inspiration to us all.

Bertha Benz: Get Up and Go Overcomes Obsessive Perfectionism

Who invented the automobile? For many historians, it is Karl Benz, but – in fact – there were so many competing inventions throughout the 19th century that no one individual can be said to be the sole inventor.

More accurately, Karl's invention, the 1885 Benz Patent-Motorwagen, was a three-wheeler but very different from the Reliants and Bond Minicars of my youth. We'll let Karl have his title as 'inventor of the automobile', but the key point is that whilst Karl was the engineer, his car is unlikely to have made it to market without the pioneering efforts of his wife, Bertha. Karl loved making constant improvements to his designs, tinkering with details, and never being satisfied that the latest was good enough or the epitome of fine engineering. Indeed, he was reluctant to let his invention see the light of day; he was the ultimate perfectionist. By contrast, wife Bertha was a pragmatist, and it was this quality which would transform Karl's endeavours.

Bertha Ringer entered the world on 3 May 1849 in the south-western German town of Pforzheim. She and Karl became engaged in 1870, and they did not appear to be a perfect match. She was attractive, well-turned out and photogenic. By contrast, Karl, five years older, appears awkward in front of the camera, sporting a huge moustache which was old-fashioned even by that era. She came from a wealthy family, attended a boarding school where she showed great interest in engineering, but was unable to progress to study this at university because of society's restrictions at the time. If it had not been for her wealth, would Karl have ever been able to develop his vehicle?

A Sunday outing changes the automotive world

Karl dithered over his 1885 patent, obsessed with adjustments for the next three years. By the summer of 1888, Bertha had had enough. Early one Sunday morning, she grabbed her two sons, Richard and Eugen, bundled them into (or, more accurately, onto) the car and set off from her Mannheim home to visit her parents in Pforzheim, nearly 70 miles south. This was a tricky journey for a variety of reasons.

For a start, these new-fangled motorised wagons were deemed illegal by the local authorities, so Bertha had to be on the lookout for police patrols. Secondly, not surprisingly given the lack of an automotive industry, there were no filling stations – there had never been any such demand. For a vehicle capable of only 25mpg, how was Bertha going to refuel the 1.3-gallon tank to reach her destination, never mind the return journey? So, a local pharmacy (in Wiesloch) took the unexpected honour of becoming the world's first filling station. Bertha purchased their entire stock of ligroin, a petrol derivative used for cleaning. Good job it was open on a Sunday.

Pragmatism wins over perfectionism

How reliable was the vehicle? Inevitably, it was untested, and Bertha was about to become an early DIY mechanic. The wooden brake blocks soon wore down, so Bertha persuaded a local shoemaker to attach leather strips to the blocks – ingenious. The fuel line became blocked, so she used her hatpin to remove the sediment. Evaporating water threatened to overheat the engine, so frequent stops were made to refill the system with river water. And, shockingly, for the morals of the time, she removed her garter to improvise insulation on a spark plug.

In the meantime, what about Karl? He had awoken to an empty house and no car. Frantically, he telegraphed Pforzheim to ascertain Bertha's safety. She made it there, telegraphed him back and returned five days later by a less hilly route, letting Karl know in no uncertain terms that the vehicle needed an additional gear for climbing hills.

But this journey was transformative – it displayed Bertha's no-nonsense, courageous spirit; it proved that the car worked and had prospects; and it transformed society's view of motor transport. Although the trip was secret, there were plenty of people en-route who observed the car and its passengers. News spread rapidly by word of mouth from those who were both awestruck yet reassured by the sight. No longer to be feared as an illegal appliance, condemned as blasphemous by the Vatican, the automobile caused excitement and aspiration for the future.

A strange future loomed for the Benzes, though. Karl would die in in 1929 and thus did not see the rise of the Nazi party, but Bertha lived till May 1944 and became an admirer of Hitler. The governing Nazi party lauded her as 'a brave German mother', something which her 1888 expedition with her children in Karl's invention certainly demonstrated, although maybe not quite in the way the propagandists meant. As always, we need to distinguish an individual's achievements and work from the excesses of their personality.

In 2008, Bertha's route became the official Bertha Benz Memorial Route, incorporating the site of the 'world's first filling station'. Bertha's principal achievement is that she showed what could be achieved with energy, pluck, determination and a disregard for convention.

Nils Bohlin: The Ultimate in Design Altruism?

Which safety feature in a road vehicle has been the most effective? Disc brakes? Airbags? Radial-ply tyres? For many motorists, family members and engineers, the answer would be very clear – the three-point seatbelt.

Prior to the three-point system, seatbelts had been available to drivers and passengers for many years, but essentially as two-point systems lying across the lap and fixed to the floor on either side of the seat. Used in cars essentially only by racing drivers, they restrained the abdomen and prevented the whole body from flying forward in a high-speed impact, but could still cause extensive abdominal injuries by crushing organs. Nor did they prevent upper-body or head injuries.

From ejection to retention

Nils Bohlin's invention was to change all this. Born in July 1920 in the south-west of Sweden, his family moved to a larger village in Dalarna, where he attended high school in Falun. Gaining a Bachelor of Science degree, Bohlin worked initially for the aircraft division of Saab, designing ejector seats for fighter aircraft. This was in the 1940s, when pilots were used to being shot down in warfare (although Sweden was neutral) and needed to escape rapidly. Fascinated by the challenges of safety engineering, Bohlin rose to become Saab's first chief safety engineer. Pilots were accustomed to wearing four-point seat-harnesses with two shoulder straps attached to the rear of the high-backed seat. In his aeronautical work, Bohlin was focused on keeping occupants safe while under the extreme acceleration of ejecting when they were catapulted rapidly out of the cockpit.

By contrast, his next job focused on keeping occupants safe whilst under extreme *de*celeration. In 1958, he was recruited by Volvo Cars, and the company was renowned – even then – for its commitment to safety, a matter prioritised by the death in a motor accident of a family member of the company's chairman. Bohlin knew that the four-point harness system would not work in a car because it restricted access to the rear seats and prevented drivers from swivelling their bodies when reversing the vehicle. So, he came up with a three-point system, comprising a lap belt with a shoulder strap – known as the lap and diagonal belt.

Keeping it simple for the customer is key

For Bohlin, the absolute key to persuading car occupants to use a seatbelt was simplicity of use.

"I realised both the upper and lower body must be held securely in place with one strap across the chest and one across the hips," he once said. "The belt also needed an immovable anchorage point for the buckle as far down beside the occupant's hip, so it could hold the body properly during a collision. It was just a matter of finding a solution that was simple, effective and could be put on conveniently with one hand."

It was so simple to use that even a child could click the buckle into place, something important to Bohlin, who by now had children and stepchildren and, in due course, 11 grandchildren. The ingenuity of his design was that the webbing was anchored below the seat in a

V-shape pointing at the floor. Significantly, because the buckle was at the side, it would not cause injury. Even under extreme pressure, the belt would remain in place.

At this stage, the 'static' seatbelt was fixed in its length, and users adjusted the size by pulling on a tab, just as with aircraft seatbelts today. The 'inertia-reel' belt, allowing movement until the reel was under pressure, came later (in the 1960s) from other manufacturers; pre-tensioner devices came in the 1980s.

Volvo introduced the three-point system in 1959 to the front seats of their Volvo 544 (and subsequent models). This was within a year of the famously camera-shy Bohlin having been appointed to his role – a significant achievement both for the company and the inventor. Essentially, whilst others had invented seatbelts earlier, Bohlin made the design work effectively and simply. In his own words:

"In a way, my design works as much because the belt is comfortable for the user as it does because it is safer."

Automotive altruism

In 1969, Bohlin was promoted to head up automotive safety research across Volvo, retiring in 1985. What was even more remarkable about his design was that Volvo (with Bohlin's blessing) altruistically made the patents of the invention freely available to other vehicle manufacturers. Volvo calculated that the design had more human value as a life-saver than it did as a commodity to license. Before long, the fitting of seatbelts for both front and rear occupants was compulsory across most countries. Wearing them is now usually mandatory. When Bohlin died in 2002, one of his stepsons, Gunnar Ornmark, commented:

"Letters arrive all the time, from all over the world, thanking him for his invention; it warmed his heart very much." [1]

At the time of his death, three years after he had been inducted into the Automotive Hall of Fame, Volvo estimated that more than one million lives had been saved by the seatbelt. Today, it is far more than that figure.

Nils Bohlin (right), 1958

[1] *New York Times.* Nils Bohlin, 82, Inventor of a Better Seat belt. Obituary, 26 September 1982.

Violette Cordery: Motoring Endurance Trials Stalwart

As Bertha Benz (p8) illustrated, proving that early cars were reliable, durable and safe was a crucial aspect of their development. Several decades later, Violette Cordery was to ensure that, in her hands, several British-built brands were able to demonstrate their worth.

Born in 1900 into a Surrey family with motoring connections, Violette was to make her own mark both as a racing driver and as an endurance specialist, sufficient for her to be nicknamed 'Queen of Motorists' and 'The Long-Distance Lady'. But how did this young woman achieve these titles? By all accounts, she was a shy and unassuming child, characteristics not usually associated with derring-do and pushing the boundaries. Photos and movies of Violette portray a rather hesitant, ill at ease subject for the camera.

A teenage champion

Violette's elder sister, Lucy (from her father's first marriage), married Sir Noel Macklin, who was to become the founder of several sports car companies, including Invicta (see also Donald Healey, p49) and Railton. Macklin, a Royal Navy Volunteer Reservist, had sustained injuries in the First World War and hired the 18-year-old Violette to drive his cars in events at the nearby Brooklands track. By 1920, she was winning at Brooklands and participating in hill climbs. She became the first female to attain any record at Brooklands, averaging 49.7mph in May 1921.

With the launch of his new Invicta brand in 1925, Macklin was keen both for brand publicity and to demonstrate the car's speed and endurance. In 1926, Violette was part of a six-driver team (the other five drivers being males) to drive an Invicta at the Monza track in Italy. Over eleven and a half days, she drove for three hours at a time, followed by a two-and-a-half-minute break, often driving longer than her male counterparts. They averaged 56.47mph over 10,000 miles, breaking a series of records: 10,000 miles, 15,000 km and 20,000 km. The Italian crowds loved her determination, perseverance and guts, and on her return to London, she was showered with bouquets of flowers.

Around the world in an Invicta

Further track awards followed, but Violette's most memorable achievement was a five-month endurance drive in 1927. Having just recovered from a bout of paratyphoid fever, she took the wheel of a new, specially-modified 3-litre Invicta, in which she drove across Europe, Africa, India, Australia, the USA and Canada at an average speed of 24.6mph. A British Pathé film clip 'Woman Driver's Daring Trip' of her departure from her Cobham home can be found on YouTube, and displays how loaded the car was.[2] Not surprisingly, the chassis had been strengthened. Again, like the Monza team, she was not alone – she was accompanied by her trusted mechanic, Ernest Hatcher, her close friend Eleanor Simpson (who was also a qualified nurse), and an RAC Observer. She permitted each passenger just 20lbs of luggage. Her own 'essentials' included five evening dresses and four hats. The Invicta was also modified to create fold-down beds for when hotels (and evening dresses) could not be used, together with a pull-out side canopy under which the two men could sleep. On her return, Lord Dewar, one of the trip's supporters, commented at the celebratory reception at Hyde Park Hotel that: "*The hand that rocks the cradle will soon rock the ship of state.*" Sexist though the statement was, it recognised the strides Violette had made in female emancipation.

---

[2] (https://www.youtube.com/watch?v=Nc7KiVgBhgo)

Racing links continue post-retirement

Competition wins continued for Violette, but she was now also developing an interest in flying. It was during her training that she met Johnny Hindmarsh, whom she married quietly in 1931. In 1935, Johnny was one of a small team supporting John Cobb's world land-speed record attempt runs in a Railton, at Bonneville Salt Flats in Utah. Sadly, test pilot Johnny was to be killed in a Hawker Hurricane near Brooklands in September 1938, just short of seven years into their marriage. Reportedly, Johnny was overcome by carbon monoxide fumes in the cockpit, and the aircraft nose-dived into an empty house at 400mph. With that tragedy, Violette pretty much disappeared from public view to raise her young family.

Connections with motor racing continued for Violette, though. Her brother-in-law, Noel Macklin, who had launched her driving career in his cars, became father to future Formula 1 driver Lance Macklin (1919-2002), whilst her elder daughter, Susan, married the famous racing driver Roy Salvadori (1922-2012). Violette continued to live quietly in Surrey until her death in December 1983, aged 83.

Tony Crook: Eccentric Ex-racer Turned Car Salesman and Marque Owner

Born in 1920 into a wealthy family in Manchester, Tony Crook was a boarder at the elite Clifton College public school in Bristol. As a pupil, he owned a car, which was strictly against school rules. Driving the supercharged MG PA sports car around the affluent Clifton neighbourhood, he tried to keep his little secret by donning a false moustache. One day, he had the misfortune to be refuelling at a petrol station when the Headmaster pulled in. Expecting a thrashing (something he was used to), he persuaded a local pharmacist to supply him with an anaesthetic for his posterior – and prayed that the Head would deliver the beating before the anaesthetic wore off. What didn't wear off was his long-time connection with the city.

From Clifton College, Crook progressed to Cambridge University, later joining the RAF, where he trained as a fighter pilot. The owner of both an Alfa Romeo and a BMW 328, Flight Lieutenant Crook's passion for land and air speed would serve him well in his future career. Post-war, he became a successful racing driver, even gaining a podium place at the 1952 Monaco Grand Prix. Of all the cars he raced, his favourite was a Bristol, who had also supplied the engine of his Monaco winner.

Tony Crook in a Cooper Bristol, 1953

Retiring after a racing accident at Goodwood in 1955, Crook focused on his garage business. As a dealer, he really admired the Bristol 400 coupe, a bespoke 'gentleman's express', crafted in Bristol by the Bristol Airplane Company at their Filton airfield factory. When the parent company ran into financial difficulties and was absorbed into aircraft conglomerate BAC, Crook became a 40% part-owner of the car company in 1960, extending this to full ownership control in 1969.

This is where his unique approach both to selling cars and running a prestigious marque came in. Bristol sold all their cars through a single showroom in Kensington, London. Bristol cars were famously sleek in design, with high build standards, and they sported a BMW engine. The 406 still looked modern and refined, but Crook used his association with the UK importer of

Chryslers to install a Chrysler V8 engine into the 1961 Bristol 407 and all subsequently numbered models. A lovely burgundy 410 was driven by Inspector Lynley in the eponymous TV series.

Selecting his customers carefully

Crook was very particular about who he sold cars to – if he didn't like the look of you, then you would be ushered from the Kensington showroom and told not to return. Potential customers who received this brush-off included film director Michael Winner. Nor did Crook take to most motoring journalists, instead gaining a reputation for being rude and blunt with many of them. Those who did succeed in persuading him to loan them a test car, but were less than glowing in their reviews, received similar treatment. Reportedly, Crook's office Rolodex card index contained the word 'No' – annotated 40 times in bold green ink – against one miscreant journalist. But those journalists he took to found him charming, amusing and generous – it's just that many people never saw this side of this prickly yet kindly man.

Crook had unusual marketing techniques. Allegedly, at one motor show, he employed people to look scruffy and emit noxious smells on the Rolls-Royce stand, thereby putting off potential customers. He is also said to have dressed as a Sheikh and pretended to buy every car on another competitor's stand. His own preference was to sell new models to a small band of existing customers rather than seek new customers, a tactic which worked well until the 1970s oil crisis, when many customers' needs changed.

Bristol cars were famed for fine engineering and powerful progress, coupled with dignified appearance, the interiors decked out with plush leather upholstery and walnut trim. Quirks of design included a spare wheel located under a hinged panel in the long front wing. There was plenty of room as the panels enclosed the mighty V8 engine, a powerhouse which continued right through to the last model built in 2011, the Blenheim.

The world moves on

Crook would fly down to Filton by private plane to oversee new designs. But by the close of the century, Bristols were becoming dated and lacked the technological features that modern-day buyers demanded. When the company hit financial problems, Crook was forced in 1997 to sell half the business. An undignified slow demise followed, with Crook being ousted from the board of the new part-owners, and he was humiliated when, in 2007, they changed the locks to the showroom doors. It was no way to treat the maverick who, virtually single-handedly, had kept the marque afloat.

Ultimately, Bristol became the servicing agent and restorer of the cars they had lovingly built over previous decades. Crook died in 2014, aged 93, but the Bristol Owners' Club survives, fiercely loyal to the qualities for which the marque stood.

William Knox D'Arcy: A Global Tycoon Who Liked to Flaunt his Wealth

Why did a Welsh village come to be named after an Anglo-Australian man of Irish descent with a French-sounding surname? And how did this man grow to be successful in business in three regions of the world?

Born in Newton Abbot, Devon, in 1849, D'Arcy attended Westminster School in London until moving to Australia when his solicitor father became bankrupt. Down under, his father did well and, after studying law, young William joined his father's mining company.

The breadth of the cultural mix increased as he married, in a Roman Catholic Cathedral, Elena Birkbeck of Anglo-Mexican heritage, who was herself descended from the Birkbeck Quaker family who founded Birkbeck College, now part of London University.

D'Arcy's gold mining interests in Australia and later New Zealand made him rich enough to move in 1889 to London. Here, he bought several properties: a mansion in Stanmore, Middlesex, a country estate in Norfolk, and a London townhouse. To crown his show of wealth, he bought a private stand at Epsom racecourse, the only other one besides King Edward VII's. However, such ostentatious displays of wealth did not impress his wife, Elena, who reckoned that all the '*flattery and success has turned his head*'. She went as far as to claim that all the '*misery and unhappiness*' of her life was directly attributed to D'Arcy's wealth. Unsurprisingly, the marriage collapsed.

Persian pursuits

By 1900, D'Arcy diversified into funding oil prospecting in Persia (subsequently known as Iran) and, the following year, established the 60-year-long D'Arcy Concession. This gave him the exclusive rights to extract oil across the whole of Persia, except those regions bordering Russia, giving the state 16% of the profits – an arrangement which was to last beyond his death until 1952.

Initial exploration cost far more than D'Arcy had reckoned for. By 1905, he was seeking further funding by establishing the Concession Syndicate with Burmah Oil. Financial troubles continued, with D'Arcy hovering close to bankruptcy. In May 1908, to stave off collapse, instructions to halt exploration were given. Fortunately, these were ignored on-site and, at the end of the month, precious oil was struck. It was the world's second-largest oil field. A new company was formed, the Anglo-Persian Oil Company (APOC). This was soon to be renamed the more recognisable Anglo-Iranian Oil Company (AIOC) of which D'Arcy became chairman and, subsequently, called British Petroleum (BP).

With the growth of motoring, the newly formed Anglo-Iranian company grew rapidly to serve the enormous rise in demand for petrol. By the beginning of the First World War, the company was looking for a location in

Britain to build a new refinery where it could process its huge imports of Iranian crude oil. D'Arcy knew that success was assured. As the war progressed, the vital nature of oil and its derivatives became apparent – the world's first mechanised war was making huge demands through the deployment of trucks at the front, buses to transport the troops, and newly-invented tanks, as well as the changeover from coal and steam to diesel-powered ships.

Creating the first national UK refinery

Planners reasoned that a site out of the range of enemy ships' guns would be safest, choosing the newly-named Llandarcy ('Llan' being Welsh for village), in Glamorgan. Nearby Swansea Bay was deep enough for the tankers to moor whilst awaiting entry to Swansea Docks. Five miles inland, behind the hills and away from enemy naval bombardment, lay the 'ideal' site. Nobody had yet thought of aerial bombardment! This lack of foresight would come back to haunt William's successors. Llandarcy, the UK's first refinery (and sometimes called 'The National Refinery'), opened in 1919, two years after D'Arcy's death at age 67. He would have been delighted with this title. It was opened by Trade Minister and future Prime Minister, Stanley Baldwin, and would produce a variety of fuels, paraffin wax, specialist oils and, latterly, bitumen till its closure 90 years later.

Alongside the refinery, the garden village of Llandarcy was built for the workers, with extensive sporting facilities still used today (and also housing the purpose-built elite training centre for the Ospreys rugby team). Perhaps this was a reminder of Elena, his first wife and her Quaker ideals – like the Quaker-owned chocolate businesses Cadbury and Fry with their workers' villages.

However, with the advent of the Second World War, the refinery was now a clear target. Significant numbers of stray bombs landed in the adjoining Crymlyn Burrows, the largest of Wales's so-called 'quaking peat bogs'. The wobbly bog, which still shakes as you walk over it, presents a stunning anomaly. Called "*a real gem in Wales's natural crown*" by TV naturalist Iolo Williams, it traps large amounts of carbon, preventing them from escaping into the atmosphere, whilst alongside lies the demolished refinery site – the former producer of oils of all kinds and inevitable emitter of pollutants.

Whether D'Arcy's large frame ever bestrode the wobbly bog is unknown – nor would he have realised the pollution caused by the 650-acre industrial site named after him. D'Arcy may not have been as well-known internationally as other oil moguls like Rockefeller or Getty, but his place in history lives on as surely as do Rockefeller Plaza or the Getty Museum.

Rudolf Diesel: Enlightened Social Reformer or Engine Designer?

In a Paris street, a plaque is mounted to a social reformer, famous in France for inventing a machine to enhance the lives of workers in small, artisan workshops. But in other nations, this same honouree is renowned for having invented an engine which transformed the powering of all sorts of transportation – road, rail and sea. Confusingly, this is the same machine, invented by Rudolf Diesel. How did this apparent anomaly come to be?

Rudolf Diesel was born to a Bavarian family in 1858 and initially grew up in Paris. With the outbreak of the Franco-Prussian War in 1870, he moved to London. From here, he was despatched by his proud father to Augsburg in Germany, so that he could learn the family's native German. From an early age, young Rudolf dedicated himself to becoming an engineer, attending a technical school. He also showed great interest in art and music and, encouraged by his 'foster father' Prof Barnickel, developed great skills in mathematical, mechanical and technical drawing, as well as becoming a keen concert-goer and an accomplished pianist who enjoyed visiting art galleries. He spoke three languages fluently and took German nationality when he became 18. From Augsburg, this handsome, gifted, Renaissance youth progressed to Munich Technical University.

The imaginative young thermodynamics engineer

Graduating with the highest degree yet awarded by his university, Rudolf had been fascinated by the lectures on thermodynamics given by his tutor, Dr Carl von Linde. He progressed to becoming an apprentice at the Sulzer Engine Works in Winterthur, Switzerland, where he set to working with ammonia as a fuel for refrigeration machines. Whilst experimenting, a severe explosion nearly killed him and, during his lengthy recuperation, he focused on developing a revolutionary engine that would not require a spark to ignite the mixture and would therefore work with any fuel. The waste-loathing young Lutheran believed strongly that there must be a more efficient engine design than steam, which wasted 90% of its fuel and converted only 10% into power. In 1881, his old tutor appointed Rudolf to manage the Paris ice-making plant of Linde AG refrigeration, and he became the company's Vice-President of Technical Matters in 1890. (Linde is still a significant corporation and is the parent company of British Oxygen.)

Rudolf's first prototype engine developed into a successful machine, patented in 1893. He developed a partnership with a company in Augsburg, Maschinenfabrik Augsburg-Nurnberg – later to become MAN, a truck company still thriving today. His first compression engine, fuelled by peanut oil, was created and presented at the Munich Exhibition in 1897.

Complexity and ingenuity

And here lies both the complexity and ingenuity of Diesel's design. He ensured that his patents did not specify any one single fuel but showed how many different fuels could be used. He used the generic term 'fuel', presenting many options – ammonia, gasoline, kerosene, soft-coal oils, pure alcohol, hard-coal oils, shale oil, illuminating gas, and coal-dust fuel. His universal fuel claim was that his engine could burn "*any kind of fuel, whether solid, liquid or gaseous*", noting: "*The use of vegetable oils for engine fuels may seem insignificant today. But such oils may become in the course of time as important as petroleum and the coal tar products of the present time.*" Indeed, Rudolf perceived vegetable oil or peanut oil to be the main fuel sources.

Dedicated to social purpose

Rudolf envisaged that his machines would be stationary, not powering vehicles. Indeed, as someone fascinated by (but not in agreement with) socialist theory, his invention's purpose was social – to ease workers' tasks. By developing a small engine, cheaper, less complex, easier to maintain and more reliable than the steam engine, Diesel thought that he could rebalance the economy, giving handicrafts a new chance and revitalising the rural world: "*It is undoubtedly preferable to decentralise small industry and establish it in the countryside instead of concentrating it in large overcrowded cities, without air, without light and without space. This goal can only be achieved by an independent machine, easy to use and maintain.*"

Rudolf became a millionaire five times over, and was invigorated by a sales tour of the USA, in which his presentations were delivered in fluent English. So grew Diesel's business, licensing the design to other manufacturers. By 1912, 50% of all sales in the USA were to Anheuser-Busch Breweries in St. Louis (brewers of Budweiser). That same year, 95% of the 'engines' were used as static machines – their use in trucks did not come till 1928 after Robert Bosch had perfected his ignition system.

But disaster lay in wait. Whilst an astute designer and engineer, Rudolf had no head for finance. He overstretched himself, not only on a luxurious house but also by relying on short-term patents. Furthermore, he was persuaded to invest in Balkan oil fields, which lost him huge sums of money. To cap it all, his health, for many years delicate because of his driven personality, began to deteriorate. Crippling gout and severe depression stifled his creativity and energy.

Mysterious death

Despite his health difficulties, a promising future seemed to lie ahead. He was invited by the board of Consolidated Diesel Manufacturing in London to discuss the possible adoption of his engine for British naval submarines. Rudolf set sail from Antwerp on HMS Dresden on the evening of 29 September 1913, having booked ahead his favourite hotel, together with dinner with his friend Sir Charles Parsons of the eponymous naval engineering firm.

Having given instructions to the steward to wake him prior to docking the next morning, no trace could be found of Rudolf. His bed had not been slept in, his nightwear was laid out, unused, on his bed, and his outer clothes were found folded neatly on a railing by the ship's stern. On his cabin desk, his diary was laid out with a small 'x' drawn on the 29 September entry.

Conspiracy theories of murder abounded. Was it German spies concerned that he would leak details of Germany's U-boat fleet? Big oil companies concerned that vegetable oil might replace their oil? British coal mine owners determined that coal should continue as the main fuel for shipping? But there was no substance to these wild theories. Was it suicide? Yet why would he kill himself? He was perceived as enormously wealthy and on the cusp of a huge deal.

A body was later found at sea, his family confirming Diesel's identity by the contents in the pockets. But the foul, putrefying body was returned to the deep so no post-mortem could be undertaken. However, the contents of a letter (misaddressed, suggesting a confused mind) indicated that he was actually close to bankruptcy. The Schopenhauer philosophy book he had been reading en route (bookmarked at the section on wealth) and his strange behaviour with his son prior to leaving, suggest suicide as a possibility.

We will never know.

Rudolf Diesel's legacy is as a supremely gifted engineer, a talented but troubled man, and a social reformer. But one aspect is intriguing. What if Diesel's initial vision of an engine powered by vegetable or peanut oil had become widely used? How might the history of the world and international wars have changed? Rather than conflict over oil-producing regions, would we have had conflict over land suited to peanut production?

Perhaps no automotive godparent has ever raised such profound questions.

John Boyd Dunlop: Smoothing The Way For Us All

We've all seen pictures of old horse-drawn trailers. Whether they were farmers' carts, stage coaches, covered wagons or the early omnibus, one thing was sure… on rough tracks and unpaved road surfaces, they would shake you around. Real bone-shakers. Not only was the springing primitive, but the wooden wheels or solid tyres were, well, solid.

Whilst Charles Goodyear had developed the vulcanising process for rubber in 1839, it still meant that tyres were solid. John Boyd Dunlop was to change all that.

A rural upbringing

Born on an Ayrshire farm in Scotland in 1840, Dunlop's childhood was relatively comfortable. The 1841 census shows him living in Dreghorn with his family and two servants. By 1851, he was living with his grandparents, the Boyds, still in Dreghorn. As a child, Dunlop would not have been aware of fellow Scotsman Robert Thomson, who, in 1845, had developed the first pneumatic tyre. Its structure was crude – an air sac wrapped in leather, with questionable durability.

The young Dunlop left rural Ayrshire to train at Edinburgh University as a veterinary surgeon. Having been raised in the countryside, he would have been only too aware of the discomfort of travelling on rough roads in poorly-sprung and solid-tyred vehicles. Working as a vet would only have emphasised this discomfort as he visited rural clients and their animals.

Having qualified, Dunlop started to practise professionally in the Scottish capital. Working here for nearly a decade, in 1867 he moved to Belfast, where he established a large and varied veterinary practice. By age 50, he'd progressed to have the largest practice in Ireland.

An inspired invention

Yet it was not his success as a vet which brought him to the attention of a wider public. Watching his son Jonny trying to master riding a tricycle, in 1887 Dunlop developed a tube from rubber, fitted with a one-way valve to prevent the air escaping. A simple solution came to him. He simply tied a knot in the end of the valve, just like we do with sealing party balloons. It was this pneumatic tyre with which his name would forever be associated.

Dunlop received a UK patent for his pneumatic tyre in December 1888 – 'the first successful pneumatic tyre' according to the blue plaque attached to his then home. He had gone into partnership with Harvey du Cros, an Irishman of French Huguenot descent. A diminutive man, du Cros had become both a boxing and fencing champion in Ireland, as well as a keen cyclist. Indeed, he became President of the Irish Cycling Association. He became the financier of the company bearing Dunlop's name, and the manufacture of the pneumatic tyre began in Dublin the following year. What fortunate timing! The invention coincided with the birth of the cycle industry in the UK, and pneumatic tyres rapidly became the standard fitment on all cycles, as well as spreading into the evolving automobile industry.

Dunlop, the vet, sells his interest in the company

By 1893, with growing sales, the Dunlop Pneumatic Tyre Company moved first to Belfast, then Coventry and, in 1900, to Birmingham, where it became the Dunlop Rubber Company. Yet, by 1896, John Boyd Dunlop had sold his interest in the company and had no direct control over how it developed. In 1916, with plenty of wartime military orders, the company established Fort Dunlop as new works where, at one stage, it employed up to 10,000 people. Closing nearly a century later as production moved overseas, the 'fort' is now a listed building – housing offices, a Travelodge hotel and a retail park.

Dunlop died at home in Dublin in 1921, aged 81, long after his retirement as a vet in 1895. He had made a considerable amount of money from selling his patent to du Cros, and he lived in the well-heeled district of Ballsbridge. However, he was not the immensely wealthy entrepreneur he would have been had he retained control of the business. He concentrated on his veterinary work and, after retirement, a drapery business. His enthusiasm had been with the scientific nature of the invention, not the business itself.

Yet his business is an example of how people around the world have heard of the brand and assumed that the company was indeed his. Long after his death, in 1939, the company diversified into many other rubber-related, Dunlop-branded products – for example, Dunlopillo mattresses, footwear and sports goods. In 2013, Dunlop's likeness was even featured in the Northern Ireland £10 note, issued by the province's Northern Bank.

These days, tyre technology has progressed enormously – radial tyres, all-weather tyres, run-flat tyres (of which Dunlop was a pioneer). Dunlop Rubber remains among the premier league of manufacturers, although today Goodyear owns the Dunlop name in Europe, North America and Australasia. But, for some car manufacturers and buyers, the ultimate in design or 'bling' is large wheels with lower-profile tyres. Whilst this allows more alloy wheel to sparkle, it reduces the amount of cushioning air in the tyres and creates a harder ride. Is design taking us backwards in passenger comfort? What would John Boyd Dunlop make of it?

Gilbern: The Dream of Butcher Giles and Former Prisoner of War Bernard

How are a butcher and a former prisoner of war (PoW) connected with a Hollywood actor and the Prince of Wales? We shall discover below that the link is a sports car.

The 1950s and early 60s saw the UK emerging from the dark days of wartime and rationing. Limited supplies of steel, glass and other raw materials meant that car designs for the most part still looked pre-war, until BMC revolutionised space-engineering with the Mini, and Ford introduced the modern-style, if conventionally-engineered, Anglia and Cortina. For sports car enthusiasts, that's where the dreaded term 'kit car specials' came in. Source your running gear from a rusted-out Ford 10 or Austin 7 and fit a two-seater glass-fibre 'special' body to imitate something like the Austin-Healey Sprite you really dreamed of but could not afford. Companies like Fairthorpe, Martin, and Rochdale made a living out of supplying such reality-check kits. And because they were kits, they avoided purchase tax, which was a key attraction for cash-strapped buyers in that era.

In South Wales, that same dream struck an unlikely pair of enthusiasts. Giles Smith was a master butcher in Church Village, near Pontypridd, whilst Bernard Friese was an engineer and former German PoW. Imprisoned in Kent, Bernard had frequently nipped over the security fence at night to visit local girl, Betty. When peace-time arrived, he married her. Having been told by his German family that there was little work opportunity for him in what was now East Germany, Bernard gained employment locally in Kent with a glass-fibre body specialist, Martin. Glass-fibre was deemed a wonder product – it was cheap, readily available, non-rusting and able to be formed into exciting and curvy body shapes. At the end of the 1950s, Bernard moved to South Wales as a washing machine engineer.

The start of a dream

Giles and Bernard met by chance in nearby Bridgend and both shared a clear vision of such a car – to which they would lend their forenames – GIL and BERN. Although they each gave a syllable to the car's name, their lives and impact were different.

Excited by their project, they designed and built the first car (based on trusty Austin A35 mechanicals) from scratch in a shed behind Giles's butcher's shop. A winch was required to lower the body from the first-floor workshop, and a pear tree needed felling to extract the car. They called on local racing driver Peter Cottrell to view and test their car. Together with a favourable road test and review by Autosport magazine in 1960, they realised that their creation was too good to be merely a one-off 'special'. So, they set about building the newly-named Gilbern GT, for which they were convinced there was a viable demand.

A Gilbern GT1800

Given the downmarket reputation of kit cars, they agreed to bite the bullet and build the cars themselves in the 'factory'. Well, not build completely – these were 'component cars'. Gilbern would build the body, paint it and install the wiring, ready for the customer to fit the engine, gearbox, wheels and various components themselves in order to avoid the aforementioned purchase tax. Because demand for key components was low, they were unable to negotiate bulk supplies of engines and gearboxes directly from manufacturers. As a low-volume company, they were forced to buy individual engine and gearbox units from local franchised dealers at full price.

Success, and a £700 loan from Giles's father, meant moving from behind the butcher's shop to a factory on an old coalmine site in Llantwit Fardre. Part of the factory building was occupied by Pat's Pickles – an appropriate name for Gilbern's future finances. Established here, they hired five staff to assemble the cars. One customer was proud Welshman, the actor and Oscar-winner Anthony Hopkins, whilst the Prince of Wales had one on loan for six weeks.

Launch of new models

Upgrading to an MGA engine increased sales, and soon a new model with a Ford V6 engine was designed: the Genie. Launched in 1966, it was a pretty car, not dissimilar in appearance to the Alfa Romeo Giulia GTA of the same era. Several variations of the Genie and, later, the Invader, were produced.

At its height, the factory was producing about 100 cars a year, mostly to professionals like lawyers and bankers wanting a quality, yet different, car. In total, about 1,000 Gilberns were produced from these most unlikely beginnings. The company continued the tradition of always being short of money, so by 1968, Giles and Bernard sold out to the Collings family. Giles stepped down completely.

Collings subsequently sold the business on to other owners when they encountered financial constraints themselves. In the process of removing the car from its creators, some observers felt that Gilbern lost its spirit. With the introduction of VAT on component cars, production ceased completely in 1974, and the Gilbern T11 mid-engined model never saw production.

Bernard becomes a successful entrepreneur

Bernard had stayed on a year to assist the transition to new owners, but an engineer at heart, he developed his design skills in new ways. He founded Morgan Marine, a glass-fibre and composite buildings company. Under him, it grew to 350 staff in Llandybie, Carmarthenshire and remains a world leader in its field. Bernard died from cancer in 2010, aged 82. Giles retired quietly, pre-deceasing his colleague in August 2003. Yet the glass-fibre body meant that many of the cars themselves remain very much alive, prized and roadworthy, and frequently displayed by the vibrant Gilbern Owners' Club.

Alma Green: She Wrote a Motorists' Guide Which Should Never Have Been Needed

A motorists' guide to where you *can* and where you *cannot* travel safely in your own country – that was the stark need for which Alma Green and her husband Victor identified a pressing demand.

From the early 1920s, increased car ownership gave Americans the opportunity to explore and travel, but African Americans were severely restricted in this apparent independence. Early twentieth-century southern states had what were called Jim Crow laws – segregation legislation which barred African-Americans from certain public spaces: hotels, restaurants, fuel stations and from even being in certain towns after nightfall. Ignore the law, and you would be subject to threats of violence – or actual violence.

As a result, between 1910 and 1940, many black Americans, 1.6 million of them, migrated north to the great industrial cities. Laws in the northern states were less draconian, but you still had to make the long journey there. Additionally, such were the constraints on leisure or business travel, that many African-Americans were accustomed to travelling with their own bedding, portable toilets, fuel cans, ice coolers and even spare car parts. This was to avoid encountering unfriendly storekeepers and hoteliers.

A childhood of poverty

It was against this horrific backdrop that Alma Green grew up. Born in Richmond, Virginia, in June 1889, Alma experienced racial prejudice during her childhood in the Jackson-Ward district of the state capital. This area was considered to be culturally-rich, with many inspirational and activist inhabitants, such as Maggie Lena Walker, the first black President of a US bank. Nevertheless, life was hard for Alma's family (two brothers, a homemaker mother and plasterer father). She attended one of the city's best black primary schools and progressed to the Richmond Colored and Normal School.

Details are unclear, but sometime in the 1890s, her mother disappeared from the records (perhaps dying?), and Alma was listed in the 1900 census as living with relatives along with her brothers. This family turbulence led to her continuing her schooling but not graduating from high school.

By 1907, the 18-year-old was working as a dressmaker, progressing to become a house-servant in 1910. Within a few years, she had joined the Great Migration north and was living in New York City, where the rest of her known family joined her – with the exception of brother William. He had died of tuberculosis in Richmond, a disease to which black Virginians were significantly more prone than whites.

The spark of an idea

In 1917, Alma became engaged to postman Victor and was married before he set off to war in Europe in 1918. On his safe return, he resumed his US Mail job. The newlyweds' families were close and they, plus friends, colleagues and the couple themselves, would experience what they delicately called:

"difficulties encountered; oftentimes painful embarrassment suffered which ruined a vacation or business trip."

Alma's younger brother, Robert, worked as a chauffeur in New York City and doubtless experienced some of these 'difficulties'. Collectively, from their apartment in Hackensack, New Jersey, the family compiled information for the 1937 first edition of *The Negro Motorist Green Book* (as it was initially titled).

For those who could afford one, a car gave freedom from the segregated transport of coaches and trains. Just as a study of bus timetables can reveal the social history of the growth of towns, so the *Green Book* unwraps the geography of those areas and services open to black travellers. And those which were indeed closed. The book shows not only the restrictions – for example, most filling stations would not serve black customers – it also acted as a means of defiance. In essence, the book indicated how to travel more safely, with Alma constantly searching for potential entries from hotels, motels, shops, garages and other services on which travellers depended.

Across the filling station network, Esso had a reputation for both welcoming black customers and recruiting black workers. In the early 1940s, 312 of the 830 Esso franchisees were black. So, it was natural that these stations would become a primary stockist of the book. It's not known how many copies of the *Green Book* were sold over its three decades from 1937 to 1966, but over that time, it grew from 16 pages to nearly 100. No records exist, but estimates place sales at around 15,000 copies each year. The National Museum of American History describes this 'atlas of self-reliance' as a tool that:

"allowed families to protect their children, to help them ward off those horrible points at which they might be thrown out or not permitted to sit somewhere."

The Green Book

Expanding the guide's scope

By 1949, Alma and Victor had established a travel agency specifically for black travellers. By the 1960s, the guide expanded to contain information on cruise ship journeys to Alaska, Canada, Mexico and the Caribbean.

Victor had already retired from his full-time job as a postman and would focus more fully on editing the book. He died in 1960, aged 67, whereupon Alma took responsibility with her mostly female staff for running the travel agency and producing future editions of the guide. It was during this period, the early 1960s, that the USA's racial tensions became not only more acute but widely known internationally. Segregation was bitterly debated and legislation to end it eagerly sought. An Oscar-winning film, *Green Book*, is inspired by the era, following a 1960s journey taken by a black pianist and his white driver across America.

Legacy

The final edition was in 1966, two years after the passing of the Civil Rights Act of 1964. With great relief to Alma, it meant that the statement below, which had appeared annually since 1948, could be realised:

"There will be a day sometime in the near future when this guide will not have to be published. That is when we as a race will have equal opportunities and privileges in the United States. It will be a great day for us to suspend publication."

Alma died in 1978, shortly before her 89th birthday. Her legacy was that she and Victor had lightened the load which black travellers and motorists took with them over many decades. Alma was inducted into the prestigious Automotive Hall of Fame in 2022.

Donald Healey: The Father of An Iconic Sports Car

The 1950s were the golden days of sports cars. Whilst the Jaguar XK140 and XK150, Porsche 356, and various Alfa Romeos were exciting and iconic as prestige examples, identifying a sports car of that era that was relatively cheap, reliable and which oozed character is more tricky. The name Austin-Healey comes to mind. Austin may have been a household name, but who was Healey?

A teenage pilot

Donald Healey was born in 1898 in the Cornish coastal town of Perranporth, where his parents, Fred and Emmie, ran a local general store. Fascinated as a boy with all things mechanical, and particularly speed, he studied engineering at nearby Newquay College. His father gained him an expensive apprenticeship in 1914 with the well-established Sopwith Aviation Company, earning Donald a princely six shillings a week.

During the First World War, Sopwith's aircraft became legendary, particularly the Camel biplane. In 1916, before his apprenticeship was complete, Healey volunteered with the fledgling Royal Flying Corps (the forerunner of the RAF). Having been economical with the truth about his age, the plucky teenager earned his wings as a pilot and went on night-time bombing raids, as well as anti-Zeppelin patrols. However, after a series of crashes, he was invalided out of the RFC, taking on the role of checking aircraft components for the remainder of the war. Less glamorous it may have been, but it sealed his focus on quality engineering.

After the war, Healey returned to his native Perranporth, where he took a correspondence course in automotive engineering and then opened a garage. The lure of the garage was to prove temporary, though – Healey was far more interested in preparing cars for rally competition. By now married to Ivy, in 1929 he entered the prestigious Monte Carlo Rally and, in 1931, won in an Invicta 4½ litre. Now was the time to move forward in his career.

Selling the garage and moving to the Midlands, Healey worked for the still independent Riley before moving to Triumph. Promoted here to Technical Director, he was instrumental in developing several sporting Triumphs, finishing third in the 1934 Monte Carlo Rally in a Triumph Gloria of his own design. The outbreak of the Second World War brought about an enforced change in focus, though, and Healey transferred to Humber, designing their famous armoured cars. This was crucial, not just to the war effort, but to Healey's future as he met colleagues with whom he would later collaborate.

Confidence to launch his own company

When the war ended, Healey established his own business, the Donald Healey Motor Company, collaborating with former Humber colleagues and utilising Riley engines. Their work culminated in the Silverstone model – but an even bigger prize was on the horizon.

A 1946 Healey Westland. Donald Healey, centre

Setting off by sea across the Atlantic for a meeting with General Motors about supplying Cadillac engines, Healey had a chance encounter with George W. Mason, the boss of car-to-refrigerator conglomerate Nash-Kelvinator. Mason warned that the General Motors meeting would fail, but should negotiations prove unsuccessful, Nash would be interested in forming an alliance to build cars. And that is what happened. The Nash-Healey was born in mid-1950, proving moderately successful. But the real value of the experience was in laying the groundwork for what was to become his most famous model, the Healey 100. Healey had long envisioned progressing from heavy, powerful, expensive cars to producing "*a very fast everyday road car with genuine sporting characteristics, capable of 100mph, which would be exceptionally cheap to buy and easy and economical to maintain*".

From Healey to Austin-Healey

The Healey 100 debuted at the 1952 London Motor Show, where a surprising twist in the tale unfolded. On the night of the opening day, Healey met Leonard Lord, head of the Austin Motor Company. Many competitors and employees fell out with Lord because of his brusque temperament, yet for Healey, it was a heaven-sent opportunity. Lord was bowled over by the 100, so much so that he purchased the rights to the car and offered Healey a production contract (which lasted till 1967). By the next morning, the show car had been rebadged the Austin-Healey 100. It would be built in the Longbridge factory, the home of Austin.

An Austin-Healey 100

Under the Austin-Healey label, other memorable cars followed. The 100 grew into the 3000 with sleeker, more confident lines and a bonnet bulge to accommodate the larger engine. Additionally, the 'Bug-Eye' Sprite became a highly popular entry-level sports car for the flat-capped, tweed-jacketed set of the late 50s and early 60s. By this time, Austin had merged with Morris, and with various other proud names, later became the home to badge-engineered BMC brands. The later Sprite and MG Midget were virtually indistinguishable apart from badging and radiator grilles, gaining the moniker 'Spridget'.

By now, Healey was Chair of the Midlands sports car company, Jensen, where he designed the famous 541S model with its huge Chrysler V8 engine and created the Jensen-Healey (1972-1976). This modern small sports car was essentially for the US market. After experimenting with various Ford, Vauxhall, and BMW engines, the notoriously unreliable Lotus two-litre engine was adopted. With a stark interior design with a plastic centre console and uniformly black interior, the Jensen-Healey sported rubber bumpers for the US market.

Donald Healey eventually retired to his beloved Cornwall, having been awarded a CBE in 1973 for services to export. His 27-acre Trebah estate near Falmouth became home to various experiments with electricity, particularly for developing nations. Healey died in 1988, aged 89, eight years after Ivy's death. In his later years, he had travelled to various Austin-Healey clubs in the USA, always amazed by the affection and enthusiasm for the cars he created. A staggering 74,000 Austin-Healey 100s had been produced, 80% of them exported.

How far does luck play in the success of a person's life? Healey was lucky in many ways – yet this is not to downplay the energy, persistence, determination and engineering skills he brought to all he did, nor the bravery he displayed in his flying missions. Beyond these powerful personal attributes, he was lucky in having supportive parents who funded his apprenticeship, lucky that his flying accidents did not result in serious injury, lucky in the chance at-sea meeting with Nash's Mason, and phenomenally lucky in meeting Leonard Lord at the Motor Show. His legacy was summed up by John Lamm in *Road and Track*: "*Jaguars were cars you dreamed of, while Austin-Healeys were affordable cars meant to be driven*".

John D Hertz: Transportation Revolutionary

Few people associated with automobiles have had such a varied range of business interests as John D Hertz. You might assume that he was born into privilege and extended his successful business reach across multiple successful companies, but that was far from the truth.

Born Sandor Herz in 1879 in part of Austro-Hungary, now Slovakia, this is the tale of a penniless immigrant to the United States who became the embodiment of 'The American Dream'. At the age of three, Herz's family sailed to the USA and later settled in Chicago. Thrashed by his father for his poor progress in school, Sandor left at the earliest opportunity, running away from home aged 12 and becoming a boxer. He adopted the name Dan Donnelly, believing that it was better to be considered Irish than Jewish. Despite having only an elementary education, he secured a job at the Chicago Morning Herald and rose through the ranks, becoming a sports writer until the paper was acquired by the Chicago Record, at which point he lost his job. Having a strong following among boxers and boxing promoters, by 1903, at the age of 24, the now-renamed

John Hertz started managing several moderately successful Chicago boxers.

Rising out of poverty

Hertz fell in love with Frances 'Fannie' Kesner but the prospect of marriage was initially doomed by her and her parents' low opinion of his chosen profession. So, at the suggestion of a friend, he became a car salesman. He and Fannie married in 1903 and, in time, they had three children (one of whom, John D. Jr., was briefly married to Hollywood star Myrna Loy). Despite hopes of sales to his many sports contacts, he was not a success – indeed Hertz allegedly had never travelled in a car until he was 26 years old! To improve his prospects, he switched dealerships, vowing to become their top salesman. Within a year, he was outselling other salesmen and even the sales manager.

Hertz was now reputedly earning a phenomenal $13,000 a year because he had several tricks up his sleeve. Firstly, he offered free breakdown service to all customers, a welcome initiative at a time when cars were notoriously unreliable. With this success, he was persuaded to join the Walden Shaw dealership (which imported French Berliet cars), whilst he also developed Shaw's very profitable cab service for Chicago citizens.

Hertz's second shrewd idea was to rent out or use as cabs all the cars he took in part-exchange. The bright yellow Hertz logo spread globally as, over time, it became the world's largest vehicle renter.

The future's bright yellow

It was a trip to Europe – witnessing the effective, polite and efficient Paris taxi service – that inspired Hertz to persuade Shaw to adopt this business model. They negotiated 'cab stand' concessions at major hotels and downtown businesses, which proved enormously successful. Except that there was a competitor in the form of the Checker Cab Company, building and operating its own fleet of cabs. Hertz reckoned that in the gloomy and dull winter weather of 'the windy city', a stand-out colour scheme for his cabs would be yellow. So, the Yellow Cab Company was born, operating its own yellow cabs by 1917. These would become synonymous with many US cities, including, of course, New York. Later, the operation would extend to building buses and trucks – a business he sold in 1925 to General Motors, and badged as GMC.

Hertz's entrepreneurship did not stop there. By 1923, he had persuaded Chicago's city authorities to install traffic lights at busy intersections to speed up traffic flow, helping his cabs. He paid for this installation himself, offering the city a two-year free deal – after which they would pay to buy them if they were successful.

1920s Chicago was home to Al Capone's mob, and cabs were no exception to turf wars, such that the bitter rivalry between Yellow Cab and Checker sometimes involved drive-by shootings. Hertz was appalled by this – indeed, he was a generous employer, paying his own workers more than competitors and recruiting the industry's first female drivers. With 2,700 Yellow Cabs operating in Chicago, it was the largest cab company in the world.

Hertz became extremely rich and was able to indulge his and Fannie's passion for horse-racing and breeding thoroughbreds. His success in the auto business was mirrored in his equine pursuits. The cab war violence continued, though, with Hertz's premises and stables being attacked and fire-bombed. Hertz had had enough and sold Yellow Cabs to Checker in a merger of sorts. Of course, Checker brand cabs in yellow became a staple of Hollywood films.

The Great Depression followed and the Lehman Brothers investment bank approached the wealthy Hertz for a bailout – he took an 8% holding in the company. His ability to turn around companies in financial trouble extended also to Paramount Pictures and TWA (Trans World Airlines).

From transportation to philanthropy

Approaching his senior years, Hertz showed no signs of retiring and bought back Hertz Rentacar in 1953. Throughout his long life, he expressed deep appreciation for the opportunities given to him by the United States. He felt such freedom was critical to his business success, and in 1957, he launched the Fannie and John Hertz Foundation, offering prestigious scholarships in science and technology. Hertz said at its launch:

'I had for some years been looking for a way to show my gratitude and love for America. Then one day I read that Russia was turning out 100 percent more mechanical and electrical

engineers than the United States. It gave me a jolt – and also an idea."

The Foundation continues to this day. John Hertz died, aged 82, in 1961. He had become one of America's greatest entrepreneurs, transforming transportation for millions of people around the world.

Major Ivan Hirst: Out of The Ruins Came Strength

At the end of the Second World War, this modest army officer was responsible for the rescue of the virtually obliterated Volkswagen plant in Wolfsburg, Germany.

The Volkswagen ('People's Car') had famously been designed at Hitler's command in the 1930s, and the design brief for Dr Ferdinand Porsche was to create and build an aspirational form of transport for ordinary German families who could then speed along the newly developed autobahn network. The reality at Volkswagen was, shockingly, rather different. Citizens' car deposits became diverted into funding the war effort, and the factory's largely forced-labour force was reassigned to manufacturing military equipment.

Nazi defeat, of course, left German society and industry shattered. The Russians were the first Allied force to enter the Wolfsburg factory but saw no potential in it; nor did the US army. The British army, by contrast, saw some potential – but not as a factory. Captain Hirst (not Major Hirst at this point) was charged with refurbishing the bomb-damaged factory to become a repair workshop for British army vehicles.

The UK motor industry wrote off the Volkswagen idea

What of the car itself? Hirst found a prototype 'Beetle' in the ruins of the factory and showed it enthusiastically to invited visitors from the UK motor industry. Some observers felt that this funny little, rear-engined, air-cooled car could have no commercial appeal or engineering success. The official British report went as far as to state:

"... *The vehicle does not meet the fundamental technical requirement of a motor-car ... it is quite unattractive to the average buyer ... To build the car commercially would be a completely uneconomic enterprise.*"

Indeed, both the Rootes Group (the manufacturer of Hillman, Humber and Sunbeam cars) and Morris Motors turned down the opportunity to develop the Beetle. Sir William Rootes (p150) was reported to have said to Hirst: "*If you think we're going to build cars in this place, you're a bloody fool, young man!*"

The captain, however, took a very different view, one that would have a global impact on the automotive industry. Hirst decided that the Wolfsburg site could, indeed, be rescued as a factory, before sending the newly painted green Beetle to British Army HQ in Bielefeld to persuade his superiors to build the car. Gaining an order for 20,000 of them in September 1945, the first 1,000 were produced by March 1946.

More than just a car

Initially, production was slow, hampered by widespread shortages of raw materials – steel, glass and rubber for tyres. All car manufacturers immediately faced these challenges after the war. The roof on early 'Beetles' was made of two sheets of steel welded together, as it was impossible to source steel in large enough sheets to press the entire roof panel. The workforce, previously slave labour, remained malnourished, so Hirst's inspired solution was to turn the factory grounds over to vegetable production.

Funds being short, Hirst's unusual approach continued when setting up a barter deal with many suppliers, with goods being paid for with completed cars rather than cash. This strategy was frowned upon by the US, which controlled the sector of Germany that housed motor manufacturers. It argued that Germany's automobile production should be suppressed for five years to avoid potential rearmament. The sceptical British government, in turn, appointed a German lawyer to run Volkswagen, aided by a military police investigation into potential black-market operations. Still showing independence of mind, Hirst refused to take orders from the lawyer, and the investigation found no trace of corruption – the paperwork was immaculate and all the cars had serial numbers.

Hirst was firmly of the opinion that, as the Volkswagen name implied, it was indeed the German people's car. His vision was that the resurrection of the factory would re-ignite industry, self-esteem, and social fabric across the nation. He was promoted to Major and by 1949, Hirst's mission was complete – the factory had been rebuilt, pressing tools were re-commissioned, an export network to Holland had been established and, with due sensitivity, he appointed a German plant manager, Heinrich Nordhoff. The factory had been transformed by Hirst but it was Nordhoff who shrewdly observed later:

"By one of the ironic jokes history is sometimes tempted to produce, it was the occupation powers who brought Hitler's dream into reality".

Later life

Throughout his life, Hirst was a supporter of the Volkswagen enterprise. He later became a senior official at the Organisation for Economic Cooperation and Development (the OECD) in Paris. During his final years of retirement in his native Yorkshire, he was seen in his eighties driving the 'new' Beetle. Playing down his own contribution, he attributed the early success of Volkswagen to effective teamwork between the British and Germans. Yet his own ability to envisage the future and, at a practical level, to see and implement solutions to problems was a major contribution to the enterprise's success.

How Rootes and Morris may have regretted the day they turned down the opportunity Major Hirst foresaw. Both companies later went out of business, only for the Volkswagen Group to become the largest-revenue vehicle manufacturer in the world, earning €325 billion in 2024.

Ivan Hirst in retirement with an original Beetle

Soichiro Honda: Powering The World With His Engines

Few countries changed so profoundly in the twentieth century as Japan. From a rural economy, dominated by an Imperial government, through several transformational wars and the after-effects of two nuclear bombs, Japan emerged as a high-tech country with iconic, global brands, yet retaining a rich heritage and traditional customs.

Soichiro Honda was born in rural Japan in 1906 and, as a toddler, developed a passion for motor vehicles, describing the smell of engine oil as a 'perfume'. He disliked school intensely, preferring throughout his life a more practical way of learning. In Japan, tradition dictated that school reports were to be returned to school, stamped by the pupil's parents with the family seal. Herein lay Soichiro's first engineering endeavour – he created a fake seal from a rubber bicycle pedal. His deception (or ingenuity?) was discovered when he started producing other seals for fellow pupils.

Adjusting from rural life to city bustle

Leaving school and home at age 15, he made his way to Tokyo. In the bustling capital, very different from his childhood surroundings, Soichiro obtained an apprenticeship in a garage. By 1928, at the age of 22, he became the proud owner of his own garage.

After dabbling in car racing, in 1937 Soichiro diversified into setting up his own company, Tokai Seiki, to produce piston rings for the established automotive manufacturer Toyota. The first batch was rejected by Toyota as being substandard, a deep learning experience for Soichiro, who refined the process and gradually built the plant to a 2,000-strong workforce. Tokai Seiki's plants were destroyed by enemy action and an earthquake in the latter part of the war, forcing Soichiro to sell what could be salvaged to Toyota for 450,000 yen. He recovered and went on to found the Honda Technical Research Institute in 1946.

The engineering maverick

Wartime had revealed Soichiro as an engineering maverick who responded well to pressure. Tokai Seiki had a military contract to build wooden aircraft propellers. Hand-carving each one traditionally took a week. Soichiro developed a system to produce two every half hour by developing high-speed milling machines which allowed mass production by unskilled workers.

Soichiro started the Honda company in 1948, a few years after the seemingly catastrophic wartime destruction of Japanese industry. The occupying powers imposed limitations on what the defeated nations could produce and, like Germany, Japan was heavily restricted in its immediate post-war industrial output. For Soichiro, this represented an opportunity, not a constraint.

The Imperial Army of Japan had a large supply of surplus, small petrol engines which had been designed to power radio transceivers. Recently married to Sachi, Soichiro was scratching his head, wondering what to give her as a gift. He attached one of these small engines to a bicycle to make life easier for her as she ran her daily errands, and his new 'motor bicycle' caught the imagination of many people who were desperately seeking greater mobility and speedier local transport. Soon, these surplus engines inspired Soichiro to create an engine bearing his own family name. By 1948, the 'Bata-Bata' (echoing the sound of the puttering motor) Type-A engine was created, complete with its tear-drop design fuel tank.

Despite two successful products to his name, the Honda company was experiencing financial problems and needed a financial manager to complement Soichiro's own engineering expertise. Takeo Fujisawa was appointed as Managing Director, freeing up Soichiro to dream, plan and experiment.

By now, onto its Type F engine, Honda was despatching engines, fuel tanks, and other parts from its Tokyo factory in cardboard boxes. Such flexibility and adaptability in engine types made Honda one of the most diversified engine builders – something it retains today, whether for generators, lawnmowers, or outboard motors.

A world-beating design

In 1959, Honda developed a 50cc small 4-stroke motorbike with an automatic gearbox and a frame manufactured from pressed steel. Morphing into the Super Cub, it became the world's best-selling motorbike, still produced today. In turn, his strapline '*You meet the nicest people on a Honda*' transformed the image of motorcyclists from leather-clad, hirsute, macho males to friendly, ordinary people dressed in everyday clothing.

Determined to win awards, Soichiro entered a team of RC142 motorbikes in the world-famous Isle of Man TT races that same year. He was demonstrating his trademark vision of achieving a dream. He failed. Yet, significantly, Honda achieved sixth place, remarkable for a newcomer. Back to the drawing board, and after two years, Honda dominated, achieving the top three positions in both the 150cc and 250cc classes. In time, Honda (along with other Japanese brands) disrupted the global motorcycle market, seeing the closure of many established brands.

From two wheels to four

But motorbikes weren't enough for Soichiro. Now was the time to enter the four-wheel market. In 1963, Honda introduced the T360 micro-truck and the S500 sports car, both compact designs tailored for the niche Japanese market. A year later, a Formula 1 car arrived, achieving success with American driver Richie Ginther.

By 1972, the Civic compact hatchback had been launched, riding on the coat-tails of the N600 'Kei' – a successful small car specifically designed for Japan's city-car regulations. The Civic was Honda's first global car, impressing markets everywhere with its efficient engine, reliability and smoothness. Built around the world, the Civic name lives on, and modern versions are still associated with lively engines and high build quality.

Soichiro remained Company President until 1973, later becoming 'supreme adviser'. His memoirs indicate a man of vision, self-knowledge and humility, apologising for his earlier occasional outbursts of rudeness to his employees, humiliating them in public and even occasionally slapping them in the face. Soichiro died in 1991, survived by his wife, but the advertising slogan of '*The power of dreams*' guided the company into the 21st century, including the launch in 2000 of the ASIMO humanoid robot.

Leslie Hore-Belisha: A Beacon of Light?

Today's regular reshuffling of Government Ministers can make it difficult to recall their names. Certain Transport Ministers stick in the mind – Ernest Marples in the late 1950s is associated with the opening of the early British motorways; Barbara Castle in the mid-60s became famous for refusing to use her official car until rear seatbelts were fitted; and Steven Norris's subsequent career in the 1990s was with various influential transport lobbying groups before he stood unsuccessfully as Mayor of London.

There is also the apocryphal story of one Minister of State for Transport in Mrs Thatcher's government whose official car broke down on a central London street. Anxious to get to his next appointment, he was shepherded by his driver to the adjacent Tube station and, upon boarding the underground train, was immediately heard to enquire where the buffet car was, much to the amusement of fellow passengers.

But Leslie Hore-Belisha? Why should he be remembered? In fact, he became associated with *three* crucial aspects of motoring, one of which still bears his name.

Born in Devon in 1893 to an influential Jewish family, his father was an insurance manager – these two aspects playing a significant part in his later life as a government minister. He was educated at the prestigious Clifton College public school in Bristol and then at the University of Oxford, where he became President of the Oxford Union. After further study in

Europe, he saw action in the First World War, leaving as a Major, before becoming a barrister and then a Liberal MP.

Speed limits and the driving test

Hore-Belisha's ministerial appointment came just at the time when motoring was becoming more widely available to the British public. Major British manufacturers had adopted production line methods to reduce costs and introduced more budget-conscious models. Shortly after being appointed Minister of Transport in the national coalition government in 1934, he was crossing a busy London thoroughfare when a speeding sports car nearly caused what he described as "*serious injury or worse.*"

Hore-Belisha introduced the Road Traffic Act of 1934, one key feature of which was to reintroduce a 30mph speed limit in built-up areas (overturning the removal of the speed limit of an Act just four years earlier). Official figures show that in 1934, road casualties were at a record high (7,343 deaths and 231,603 injuries). Half the casualties were pedestrians, and three-quarters of incidents occurred in built-up areas – something Hore-Belisha described as *"mass murder"*.

Another key feature of the Act was to make a driving test compulsory for all new drivers and to strengthen the legal requirement for insurance for all drivers. The basis of this legislation remains in place today, and it is difficult to recognise how far-reaching its introduction was. Indeed, my own father never took a driving test, having been taught to drive by his employer, Post Office Telephones, (the nationalised forerunner of BT).

Alongside the introduction of the driving test (including long-forgotten hand signals), Hore-Belisha oversaw the rewriting of the Highway Code. That, too, is still with us today, although in a much-modified form to reflect the considerable change in motoring. Published in 1931, as an 18-page 'pamphlet', Hore-Belisha expanded its scope and detail. It reflects a focus on road safety for all, incorporating advice from the Pedestrians' Association.

A Beacon of Light

1934 was a busy year for Hore-Belisha. He also introduced, as part of these measures, what we now call the zebra crossing, accompanied by a flashing beacon on each pavement. Known officially as 'Belisha beacons', these crossings with their distinctive amber globes also evolved into 'pelican' and 'puffin' crossings and have reached many parts of the world.

Given the extensive legislation and motoring changes brought about by Hore-Belisha, why did his term of office last only three years? At first glance, he would seem to be one of the most proactive and busy Transport Ministers, but by 1937, awareness was increasing of the perceived Nazi threat and how appeasement was illusory. Hore-Belisha had been warning about the possibility of war, and this perceptiveness and far-sightedness saw him appointed as Secretary of State for War from 1937 to 1940.

However, despite his popularity with the general public, he proved unpopular with some military chiefs and Cabinet colleagues. They felt that he was more concerned about the fate of European Jews than about the security of Britain. Additionally, his lack of interpersonal skills meant that he caused friction by advocating easier promotion for soldiers from the ranks to officer level and also recommending that certain 'old school' Generals be retired early. Not surprisingly, he fell out with establishment figures. Just a few months after the war began, he was sacked, the reasons for which were never fully explained. It has been suggested that senior army officers persuaded King George to demand his sacking by Prime Minister Chamberlain.

Historians now detect considerable anti-Semitism towards him, although his contemporaries at Clifton College observed that "*Hore-Belisha was quarrelsome and good manners were not his strong suit*". After the war, he became the first (and only) Baron Hore-Belisha of

Devonport, the baronetcy dying with him in 1957 when he collapsed after giving a speech.

Leslie Hounsfield: The Engineer Who Asked "Can You Afford to Walk?"

Leslie Hounsfield spent his working life inventing and patenting the products he painstakingly engineered. Some of his products gained popularity during his lifetime, while others became well-known after he left the company he founded. He registered 15 patents connected to cars, and a number of his designs were somewhat quirky. What united all of them, however, was Hounsfield's strong driving principle to make products beneficial, easy to access for ordinary people, and affordable.

Born in 1877, Hounsfield was educated at Brighton Grammar School and then Battersea Polytechnic, leaving to become an apprentice engineer at Simpsons Pumping Engines. Having shown early signs of engineering brilliance, he had gained a notable 'Whitworth Exhibition' (named after the renowned engineer Whitworth) in 1898, thereby giving him entry to the prestigious Royal College of Science.

For a while, he worked at the leading agricultural machinery manufacturer Ransomes in Ipswich. Service in the Boer War interrupted his career, but by the age of 27, he had founded Polygon Engineering in south London. Here, he researched the internal combustion engine, determined to simplify its operation and to make vehicles more accessible to the public.

Simplicity and economy are key

Before the start of the First World War, Hounsfield transferred his business, now called *Trojan*, to Croydon where, from the late 1920s, it was a well-known landmark on Purley Way.

In 1913, he proudly registered his 'people's car', a 'Utility Car' designed as affordable transport. Production was delayed until 1922, because of the outbreak of the First World War and during this time, Hounsfield used his extensive engineering skills to diversify into producing production tools and gauges.

His lightweight tourer impressed Leyland Motors sufficiently for them to take on initial production in their factory. It boasted several remarkable features, indeed some of its design was eccentric, even if he was not. It ran on solid tyres to prevent punctures, whereas other manufacturers had progressed to pneumatic tyres in the early 1900s. For simplicity, the engine had a mere seven moving parts – four pistons, two con rods and a crankshaft. With no chassis, the engine and gearbox were housed in a punt-shaped tray suspended below the seats. Above all, in line with Hounsfield's principles, the car was cheap: £125 in 1925, the same as a Model T Ford and cheaper than the £149 Austin 7. For Hounsfield, economy was crucial in everything he designed. He even devised a memorable advertising slogan – "*Can you afford to walk?*" – based on the mathematical calculation that, over two hundred miles, new shoes would cost more than the petrol consumed.

However, Hounsfield's obsession with economy was at the expense of speed. The original car would manage only 13mph, although in the 1920s, its revised version (on optional pneumatic tyres) would travel at 35mph, and the 1931 model 45mph.

A 1924 Trojan Utility Car

Generous benefactor

1931 was also the third anniversary of the opening of the Davis Theatre in Croydon. To mark the occasion, local companies were approached to contribute prizes. Every entrant to the theatre on the anniversary date would win a prize. The star prize was the new Trojan five-seater saloon, generously contributed by Hounsfield. Trojan advertised it as:

"Graceful in appearance,

Advanced in design,

Sound in construction

Reliable & comfortable in use"

...something of a departure from the usual economy slant. It is significant that Hounsfield did not donate one of his cheaper models, suggesting altruism.

Light vans were also part of Trojan's production. During the 1920s, another Croydon company, Brooke Bond Tea, bought 2,000 Trojan delivery vans, ensuring that they were a common sight across the nation. Across the world, meanwhile, economy remained a crucial aspect of sales, including in Australia. One baker in Sydney reported in 1926 that whilst he covered 25 miles a day delivering bread, it cost him less than two shillings.

In 1933, Hounsfield, now in his fifties, stepped down as Managing Director of Trojan to start another company, Tensometer, which created and manufactured precision equipment to test the tensile properties of materials. He had also designed a folding, sprung "Safari" camp-bed, which would become familiar to thousands of servicemen throughout the approaching war. It continued to be produced in the Trojan factory.

Post-war, Trojan produced only vans. The revised van, now sporting a Perkins diesel engine with a distinctive note, was an even more familiar sight and sound in the 1950s and 60s. The red Brooke Bond Tea and green Chivers' Jellies models became best-selling Dinky Toys, too. Apparently, as a toddler, I would always report to my mother when the 'Bronk tea van' was delivering to the local shop opposite our house.

Engineering influence

By the 1950s, and now retired, Hounsfield continued to focus on supporting the engineering profession generally. He had served as President of the Institution of Automobile Engineers in 1928-29, and worked tirelessly on their Council continuously for 40 years. Over that time, this dapper and erudite leader influenced its educational policy and was awarded the Institution Medal. He fully exemplified the theme of his Presidential Address, entitled "The Integrity of the Technical Man". He was also elected a Member of two other prestigious organisations: the Institution of Mechanical Engineers and Associate Member of the Institution of Civil Engineers.

Trojan continued to lead in several other ways, albeit without Hounsfield's leadership. Post-war austerity saw a rise in bubble cars, renowned for their fuel efficiency and affordability. They featured a bubble-like canopy, reminiscent of their German planemakers' origins, such as Heinkel and Messerschmitt. When Heinkel returned to aircraft production, their Kabine bubble-car was renamed the Trojan 200, manufactured in Croydon. After Hounsfield's death, the company was to become the manufacturer of the bodies for McLaren F1 cars. Bruce McLaren (p106) sadly ended his days in one of these Trojan-bodied cars.

Hounsfield died aged 80, "*still alert and full of ideas*" according to Motor Sport magazine's obituary, on the 17th September 1957. Integrity was central to his character and drove him and Trojan to success.

Mercédès Adrienne Ramona Manuela Jellinek: A Three-Pointed Star is Born

She was a young lady whose impact on vehicles is known the world over. "*Who?*" you might ask. *"I've never heard of Ms Jellinek …. what on earth does she have to do with cars?"* What follows is the intriguing tale of how someone with no direct connections with the automobile industry became synonymous with one of its principal brands. It is known globally for the prestige, refinement and durable engineering of its cars as well as the unburstable reputation of its taxis and commercial vehicles.

Let's start with her father, the Austrian entrepreneur, Emil Jellinek. Born into a wealthy family in Leipzig, he held a variety of roles in insurance in Vienna before expanding the business to Nice in the south of France. Here, he also became a successful dealer of Daimler cars. Jellinek sold upmarket models to the aristocracy and elite who wintered on the French Riviera, where they (and he) enjoyed the balmy climate and vibrant social scene. Emil was also to become the Austrian Consul-General in Nice and an influential diplomat and businessman. With some racing success to his credit, he rose to become a board member of the fledgling Daimler (DMG) company in 1900. Part of his brief was to specify – from the renowned engine designers Gottlieb Daimler and Wilhelm Maybach – a new engine for a sports Daimler. The car proved a racing sensation as the most technically sophisticated yet built.

The racy father becomes superstitious

As a proud family man, Emil had two daughters but had lost his wife Rachel four years after the birth of his young daughter. Being superstitious, he believed that, despite his wife's death, his beloved daughter was still a blessing and that her name, the Spanish for 'gracious gifts', 'grace' or 'mercies' (*mercédès*), was apt. So, Emil insisted that the new 35hp engine be named Daimler-Mercédès after his 10-year-old first daughter, as he also did with all his houses and his yacht. By 1901, DMG had trademarked the name Mercedes (without the accents), and Emil was to break into the huge US market, marketing the car to prestigious customers such as the Astors, Morgans, and Rockefellers.

With the new engine created, Emil decreed what the rest of the cars in the series would be like – a long wheelbase, a low centre of gravity and a Bosch ignition system – as well as a new 8hp model. The cars would be known as Daimler-Mercedes.

In awe of his daughter

A highlight of the fledgling motor-racing calendar was the Nice Speed Week, home to Emil and family. The new Daimler-Mercedes cars achieved four first-place finishes in the races and five second-place finishes. In doing so, they usurped the place of the previously triumphant French Panhard-Levassor brand, which withdrew before any racing began. The turmoil caused the Head of the French Automobile Association to observe ruefully the loss of the French car manufacturer's pre-eminent position: "*We have entered the Mercedes era*". So, a twelve-year-old girl had suddenly become famous in motoring circles, even though she was never to own a car herself.

In 1903, at age 50, Emil changed his name to Jellinek-Mercédès, observing: "*This is probably the first time that a father has taken his daughter's name*". From then on, he always signed himself E.J. Mercédès.

In 1926, Daimler merged with Benz to become Daimler-Benz, now calling their cars Mercedes-Benz. Consequently, the engineering genius of Benz, Daimler and Maybach became supplanted by the name of one of their dealers' daughters – just as Rolls-Royce is often shortened to the name of the flamboyant, aristocrat salesman Rolls rather than the engineer and designer, Royce. A century later, in February 2022, Daimler-Benz would be renamed Mercedes-Benz Group, thus sealing the place of the young girl in automotive history.

The gracious gifts cease

For Miss Mercédès Jellinek, life sadly did not proceed with the 'gifts' her father anticipated. From a childhood of luxury in grand houses and aboard her father's yacht, in 1909 she married Baron von Schlosser in a sumptuous ceremony. This delighted her father's aristocratic pretensions, as here was the opportunity he had been awaiting so long for – to seal his place by marriage with the 'old money' and titled classes he was used to mingling with. Mercédès had a fine soprano voice and her younger half-sister Andrée Maja recalled that:

"Mercédès was a great, smart person, and we got on wonderfully. She was theatrical and would have loved to have become an actress."

However, her new life with the Baron was doomed, and she left him and her two children to be with an impoverished artist. She was reduced from a flamboyant life in Vienna to begging for food on the city's streets in 1918 (the same year that Emil died in Geneva). Dying from bone cancer in 1929, aged just 39, she was buried close to her Hungarian-born grandfather, the former Chief Rabbi of Vienna – from which point emerges a certain irony. In the 1930s and 1940s, open-topped Mercedes cars were the favourite transport of Nazi leaders and politicians. Did Hitler and fellow-Nazis realise that they were parading around in a car named after the granddaughter of a Rabbi?

Camille Jenatzy: Electric Vehicle Land-speed Record-holder

Camille Jenatzy was born in 1868 to parents living in the Schaerbeek suburb on the north-eastern outskirts of Brussels, an area with a rich cultural mix both then and now. His Hungarian father, Constant, was the founder of Jenatzy-Pneumatique, Belgium's first rubber factory and a well-known manufacturer of tyres.

Whilst studying engineering at university, Jenatzy competed fiercely in the sport of bicycle racing (something at which fellow Belgian Eddy Merckx would excel many years later). Jenatzy was highly strung and intensely focused on whatever was absorbing his interest at the time; so obsessive and single-minded that he was sometimes dismissive of others, displaying a ferocious temper to those who crossed him. These characteristics, along with his distinctive red beard, resulted in the nickname "Le Diable Rouge" (The Red Devil). He also had a love of practical jokes, which would catch up with him later.

After graduation, his love of all modes of transportation led him to set up his factory, The General Transport Company, in France, to build battery-powered electric cars for use as Parisian taxis. He also had some racing success and became renowned for his spirited driving style. In November 1898, he won the Chanteloup hill-climb near Paris, driving one of his own cars and covering the muddy 1.8 km uphill course at an average speed of 27.3 km/h (17 mph). Infuriated that a competitor, Count Gaston de

Chasseloup-Laubat, had gained the official land-speed record for an electric car, Jenatzy challenged him. The record bounced back and forth between the two of them over the next three months prompting Jenatzy to construct a purpose-built electric vehicle to regain the title.

Jamais Contente

In April 1899, he arrived at the next speed challenge in his specially-designed *La Jamais Contente* (Never Satisfied), which boasted twin 25-kilowatt batteries (weighing half the total weight of the car) producing 68hp direct to the rear wheels. It looked extraordinary too; its alloy body, composed of aluminium, tungsten, and magnesium, was shaped like a large, blue bullet with a steering tiller.

Crouching low in his cockpit to further enhance the car's aerodynamic shape, Jenatzy exceeded the magic 100km/h barrier and reached 105.9 km/h (65.8mph). His record would stand for three whole years until Léon Serpollet, in a Gardner-Serpollet steam car, reached 120 km/h.

Jenatzy aboard the aerodynamic '*La Jamais Contente*'

Part of the secret of the car's success was its tyres. With his knowledge of tyres and rubber, Jenatzy had specified that *Jamais Contente* would sport smaller diameter tyres with a wider tread than most cars of the day. They looked more like modern tyres, and the squatter, wider tread and appearance made the car very stable. It was fortunate that he had family access to a tyre company to meet his very particular needs. Except that these weren't Jenatzy-brand tyres! Jenatzy had developed an association with the French company Michelin to supply these specialist tyres, which contributed to breaking the 100 km/h barrier.

Back to petrol

Jenatzy enjoyed further racing success in the following years (including the prestigious Gordon Bennett races in Ireland), but he abandoned making electric cars. The battery technology of the day was heavy lead-acid batteries, which had minimal range and were slow to recharge, unlike today's lithium-ion batteries.

He returned to the family tyre business and, in 1902, became a driver for the newly trademarked brand, Mercedes. It was driving one of these powerful cars that he suffered a horrendous crash at the Circuit des Ardennes in his native Belgium. His car ended up in a ditch and was destroyed. Jenatzy was to quip that he would die in a Mercedes, but continued competing as a 'gentleman driver' until 1910 before returning to the tyre business.

Meeting a prophetic end

In December 1913, Camille joined a hunting trip in the Ardennes. A sudden impulse led him to hide from his companions in a thicket where he grunted fiercely, imitating a wild boar. He must have been a good mimic because one of the hunting party, Alfred Madoux, Director of the *Étoile Belge* journal, fired a shot into the thicket. Jenatzy was badly wounded, but friends bundled him into a car and rushed him to hospital. These final hours saw a number of strange coincidences intertwine – the location of his shooting was where many of his early motoring escapades took place; the shooter was (allegedly) the husband of his mistress; and the car? It was a Mercedes. Jenatzy did not survive the journey, fulfilling his premonition about dying in a Mercedes. He was just 45.

Charles F Kettering: The Second Edison

At the beginning of the 20th century, motor cars were rudimentary in many ways. In 1900, when Theodore Roosevelt became the first US President to use one, he took extreme measures. He refused to travel by car without being followed by a horse-drawn carriage for back-up. Cars lacked the safety features we take for granted – horns, headlights, shock absorbers, speedometers, brake pedals, seat belts.

Driving involved considerable physical effort, not just to steer but even to start the engine. Drivers, or chauffeurs, used iron starting handles, which required perfect timing and a little luck. If the driver forgot to turn off the ignition before lifting the crank at the front of the vehicle, the engine could kick back, causing a wrist injury. Even worse, the car could roll forward. After a man died in 1910 from a blow to the face by a starting-handle, the head of Cadillac, Henry Leland, vowed to find an alternative starting method.

Step forward inventor Charles Franklin Kettering. Born in August 1876, Kettering grew up on a farm outside the village of Loudonville, Ohio. Fascinated by the new electrical age, it is rumoured that with the first money he ever earned ($14 for cutting wheat on a nearby farm), he bought a telephone, which he carefully dismantled, inspected, and rebuilt. This practical, down-to-earth personality was coupled with a sharp, innovative mind, though. After graduating from high school, he taught in a one-room schoolhouse near his home and was remembered as a tall and well-built individual, and an inspiring teacher who put 'learning through practice' at the heart of all his teaching.

Patient and determined

Kettering entered college twice, in 1896 and 1898, but both times he had to return to teaching because constant studying was ruining his eyesight. With determination and perseverance, he eventually graduated, aged 28, in mechanical and electrical engineering from Ohio State University.

Electricity was now transforming home life, industry, and agriculture, and Kettering wanted to be part of this revolution. Upon graduation, he was immediately recruited as an experimental engineer at the National Cash Register Company (NCR) in Dayton, Ohio. During his five years there, he created a low-cost printing cash register, an electric cash register (with a small electric motor to open the drawer), an accounting machine for banks, and a system that allowed sales clerks to check a customer's credit quickly. He also had a side hustle, developing a better ignition system for automobiles.

Transformative inventions

In 1909, together with NCR's general manager, Colonel Edward A. Deeds, Kettering founded the Dayton Engineering Laboratories Company (soon to be known, as it is today, as Delco). The company's aim was to improve the automobile with electrical systems. Within three years, Kettering and his colleagues had designed and built all-electric starting, ignition, and lighting systems for automobiles. Specifically, he invented the electric starter in 1911, a device which would transform motoring across the world. Adopted first by Cadillac, the electric starter soon became available on other brands. With this invention, cars became not just easier to start, but also benefited women, who could now drive independently. In 1916, Delco became part of United Motors Corporation, an automotive parts and accessories company. Its President was Alfred Sloan (p.161), with whom Kettering would later work extensively.

"It doesn't matter if you try and try and try again, and fail. It does matter if you try and fail, and fail to try again."

United was acquired by General Motors in 1918, and Kettering became the head of the new General Motors Research Corporation in Dayton, becoming a vice president of GM in 1920. In 1925, the research laboratories were relocated to Detroit, prompting Kettering and his wife to move to the city, where they lived in a Renaissance-style hotel until his retirement. He remained head of General Motors Research for 27 years, acquiring an astonishing 186 patents in his name. His other notable creations include the development of ethyl leaded gasoline, the development of the refrigerant Freon (his home, after retirement, was the first in the USA to be air-conditioned), the development of faster-drying and more durable lacquer finishes for automobiles, and the creation of the lightweight diesel engine.

Away from the automobile industry, Kettering was firmly of the belief that electricity could enhance the healthcare of patients. Consequently, his medical inventions included an incubator for premature babies, a treatment for venereal disease, and magnetic diagnostic devices.

Over the decades, it became clear that some of his inventions, such as adding lead to petrol to reduce 'knocking' and devising CFC refrigerants were actually harmful ecologically, but plainly this was not realised at the time.

In 1937, Ohio State University's Robert Derrenberger (see bibliography) was to write that Kettering spoke:

"with sparkling vitality, yet never with a waste of words. His manner is friendly and free from any suggestion of dominance.

Ohio State University is proud of Charles Kettering and this magazine welcomes the opportunity to pay tribute to him whom we all think of as America's second Edison."

Philanthropy

Kettering was also the inspiration behind the creation of an engineering college based on practical education in which "*the theory should supplement the practice and not precede it.*" It was called the General Motors Institute.

He also founded (with Alfred P. Sloan) the Sloan-Kettering Institute for Cancer Research in 1945. His greatest honour came in 1998, though, when the General Motors Institute was renamed Kettering University after "one of the century's greatest inventors."

To quote Derrenberger again:

"Perhaps the most unusual thing about Kettering is his patience and his systematic way of thinking. When a problem is given to him, he takes it apart, finds out the cold facts and then works out the solution. He is a thinker who goes straight through prejudice and fog and always ends with a sane conclusion."

Kettering retired from General Motors in 1947 but remained a research adviser until his death, after several strokes, in November 1958 in Dayton. Kettering summed up his career appropriately when he mused, "*My interest is in the future because I am going to spend the rest of my life there.*"

Frederick W Lanchester: A Genius Inventor and Engineer

Frederick Lanchester ably fits the description of a little-known motoring hero. His achievements were many and varied, as befits a polymath, yet few people today will be familiar with his name or the designs of this highly respected engineer. How could a genius have ended up in near-penury?

Frederick was born in St John's Wood, North London, in 1868, one of eight children to parents Henry, an architect, and Octavia, a Latin and Maths tutor. His parents' professions played a crucial role in shaping the extraordinary talent he developed as someone fascinated by the interconnection between mathematics, design and language. Two of his brothers, George and Frank, were also closely involved in his engineering and business activities and have a rightful place in automotive and aeronautical history, too. Other siblings became a notable suffragette (Edith) and an architect (Henry).

A late developer

Relocating as a child to Brighton, Frederick was packed off to preparatory school, then boarding school. He hated them, reflecting as an adult that "*it seemed that Nature was conserving his energy*". As a late developer, he won scholarships to two institutions which later became part of top-class engineering and technology universities: Southampton and then Imperial College, London. Alas, he left both without qualifications, although he was awarded an Honorary Doctorate in 1920 from Birmingham University.

Working initially for the Post Office, Lanchester developed a patent for a draughtsman's device. His 'isometrograph' helped draughtsmen draw parallel lines, an essential task in many types of design and technical drawing.

He continued to design and patent for various companies a variety of devices, such as a wick carburettor, a pendulum governor, and a pendulum accelerometer. The success of these designs and patents across a wide range of engineering disciplines – aeronautics, engine design and boat design (he designed the first motorboat built in Britain) – set an unfortunate precedent. Frederick was frequently unable to turn any of his ingenious and innovative designs into money-making concerns. An exception was the self-starting device for gas engines, which he sold for a handsome figure. He had deleted the clause in his employment contract stating that intellectual property rights belonged to his employer. Why was he not savvy enough to do something similar with other contracts?

Astounding breadth of achievements

Even listing just a handful of Fredericks' inventions is hugely impressive. From 1892, before the Wright Brothers' first powered flight, Frederick became absorbed with studying aeronautics, inspired by watching the flight of herring gulls whilst on a transatlantic voyage. Upswept wings and theories about aerodynamics followed.

Discouraged by the emerging aero engineering profession's dismissive attitude to his theories, Frederick transferred his attention to motor vehicles. He was a visionary genius, responsible for many significant inventions and developments in automotive engineering. These included: disc brakes, an 'automatic' transmission system, power steering, four-wheel drive, fuel injection, the dynamic balancing of engines and low voltage ignition.

Over his life, Frederick Lanchester filed an astounding total of 426 patents. He also established the Lanchester Engine Company and the Lanchester Motor Company. In 1895, he designed and built the first all-British four-wheeled motor car. He also worked for Daimler, as well as designing the engine for the Mark V tank, and the Lanchester Armoured Car.

Preferring research to management

Growing tired of managing the Lanchester companies, Frederick left them in the hands of his younger brothers, George and Frank. His constantly active mind much preferred research and development, so he became technical consultant to Daimler, with whom he would have a long-standing relationship. In due course, the Lanchester Motor Company was acquired by Daimler, which itself was subsequently absorbed into Jaguar in 1960.

As if this were not enough, under the pen-name Paul Netherton-Herries, Frederick was a poet, publishing two volumes of work privately rather than through an established publisher. He had a fine singing voice and was also a friend of writer Rudyard Kipling, periodically sending him new inventions to test out.

Lanchester's genius gained him many awards: he was elected a Fellow of both the Royal Society and the Royal Aeronautical Society, and was awarded gold medals from the Institution of Civil Engineers and the Institution of Mechanical Engineers. In 1909, he became a member of Asquith's Advisory Committee on Aeronautics where, ironically, some of his views were rejected as too advanced – for example, predicting that aircraft might play a role in a future war.

With a heavy workload, his health suffered. He developed Parkinson's disease, and the rigours of this debilitating illness, together with the worsening effect of two cataracts, meant that he was unable to take on any official work during the Second World War. As he recalled later in life:

"My work has been almost wholly individual. My scientific and technical work has never been backed by funds from external sources to any material extent, or been assisted by the holding of a position such as would give me command of any material resources. All research work that I have done was paid for out of my own pocket."

Post-war, Frederick lived in straitened circumstances, unable to earn a living. He died in 1946 in the Birmingham house he had designed himself in 1924. He was only able to continue living in his home thanks to charitable help.

Legacy

After his death, the final Lanchester saloon was a badge-engineered version of the Daimler Conquest – cheaper and with a smaller engine. It was a sad way to mark the passing of such an innovative and inspiring designer.

In his adopted workplace of Coventry, during the 1970s, several colleges merged to form Lanchester Polytechnic, which had a fine name for its own engineering courses. In time, it became Coventry Polytechnic and, today, is Coventry University. A key building in the university's heritage is the Frederick Lanchester Building, a uniquely designed structure that also hosts an engaging online, interactive resource about Frederick.

In Birmingham, on the very site where Lanchester built their original petrol, four-wheel car in 1895, is a sculpture, the Lanchester Car Monument, unveiled by his niece Marjorie Bingham in 1995.

Dorothy Levitt: Media Sensation of the Early Motoring Era

Dorothy Levitt had a meteoric rise to fame in the early twentieth century. Born to a wealthy Jewish family in the East End of London, her father had anglicised the Levi surname to Levitt.

In 1900, she was appointed, aged 18, as a typist for the engineering company Napier, which had recently diversified into building luxury cars. Here she caught the eye of Selwyn Edge, a director of an associated company. He singled her out because of her good looks to train as both a driver and mechanic.

As Napier's leading racing driver, Edge saw Levitt's roles as essential to attract potential interest from women in driving – and buying – cars. He also found Levitt quite irresistible, *"A beautiful secretary with long legs and eyes like pools,"* according to one account, and she became his PA, both of them having a penchant for self-promotion. She seems to have formed a romantic as well as a work association with Edge, disappearing from home and evading the arranged marriage her parents had lined up for her.

Levitt took to the car roles immediately, despite the protestations of her driving tutor, apprentice Napier salesman, Leslie Callingham. He had been dragooned into teaching her, but was firmly of the opinion that women should not be in the driving seat.

"The fastest girl on earth"

Selwyn Edge was the UK agent for Gladiator cars, and it was this brand for which Levitt initially drove. In

1903, she became the first woman to compete in a car race and took her first chequered flag later that year. By 1905, she had set the record for the longest drive by a woman, from London to Liverpool in a single day (returning the next day). Setting a new world speed record for women of 91 mph at Blackpool, she became known as "*The fastest girl on Earth.*" Often, she was photographed driving with her black Pomeranian dog, Dodo, by her side.

As Levitt's racing successes burgeoned, including in speed trials and hill climbs, her media profile rose. She diversified into racing boats between 1903 and 1908, gaining awards in this new field through her skill, bravery and determination. She also stated that she was to become an aviator, but there is no evidence that she actually attained her licence.

Levitt's newfound fame led her to write articles about motoring, becoming seen as the voice of the female motorist. So much so that it is reported she became driving tutor to Queen Alexandra and her Princess daughters. Again, the evidence for this royal link is scant. By 1909, Levitt had written a book, the quaintly-named *The Woman and the Car: A Chatty Little Handbook for All Women Who Motor or Want to Motor.* Here she dispensed useful advice to female drivers on choosing, purchasing, driving and maintaining a car – some of it sensible, some rather odd. Advice included carrying gloves to protect from the elements; using chocolate as a long-lasting, non-perishable energy boost; and, of course, under the driver's seat, women should carry a revolver (preferably a Colt 45 because of its compact size). Advice on using a long-handled mirror to periodically observe what was happening behind is a reminder that cars had few of the features we now take for granted. However, Levitt did not always follow her own advice – her personal preference for driving outfits was not functional. Rather, she sported fashionable, shapely clothes (ready for any photo opportunity) covered by a duster coat.

It was in motoring that Levitt attained some notoriety. In November 1903, she received a speeding summons for racing through Hyde Park. Her defence was not helped by admitting that she regretted not running down and killing the arresting police officer. Separately, the very same month, she became the first person to win a motoring law case, against a GPO delivery driver who had struck her vehicle.

From fame to obscurity

In 1904, Levitt suffered unspecified ill health and was advised by her doctor to recuperate in the warmer climate of Madeira. Not an easy sea trip in those days.

Back in the UK, Napier wound up its sporting operations in 1908, and Edge had little further professional need of Dorothy Levitt. Interestingly, her 1909 book makes no mention of him at all, suggesting a souring of the relationship. Levitt disappeared from public view around 1910, even from the electoral roll.

Nothing more was heard of Levitt until her body was found in her Marylebone house on May 17, 1922, some dozen years later. The death certificate recorded death due to "morphine poisoning while suffering from heart disease and an attack of measles". The inquest concluded with a verdict of misadventure. With a passion always for the seaside, she was buried in

Brighton's Jewish cemetery, where her gravestone erroneously records her age at death as 39, not 40.

Dorothy Levitt in a 26hp Napier at Brooklands, 1908

Rev. Peter John Lunati: The Mechanic Who Gave a Lift to The World

Many of the characters featured in this book have been driven by strong principles – engineering, organisational, a mission for sales, or an altruistic desire to enhance the quality of life for others. Peter Lunati, whilst of a mechanical frame of mind, was inspired by his Pentecostalist religious faith.

Lunati, born 16 July 1890, was an Italian-American automobile mechanic from Memphis, Tennessee, where he grew up working on motor cars. During the First World War, he was posted to France, serving both as a mechanic and a spiritual adviser. After war service, he returned to Memphis and opened a service station.

Peter in the pits

Repairing and servicing cars had moved on from the early days when mechanics scrabbled under cars, spanners in hand, to carry out work. As cars became more popular, they also became more complex machines with lower ground clearance, as they now had smaller wheels than their predecessors. Crawling underneath, even with a rudimentary jack to lift the vehicle slightly, was precarious, uncomfortable and inefficient. So, the inspection pit was born – a dugout accessed by steps or a ladder to enable the mechanic to view and work on the underside more easily. That was only a partial solution – mechanics still had limited light and, if they needed a particular tool, they had to climb out again. It wasn't good for the knees! Nor did all garage floors lend themselves to such excavation.

Certainly, Lunati was growing tired of this clambering around. One day, whilst getting his hair cut, he noted the ease with which the barber's chair could be raised and lowered to the desired height. It could be swung around through 360 degrees to optimise light on the customer's head. A simple foot action by the barber controlled all the movement hydraulically with minimal effort. Why could this pump principle not be applied to raising cars? For Lunati, it was also important to be able to rotate a car so that it never had to be reversed within the garage.

So how does a hydraulic lift work?

In 1653, Blaise Pascal, the French scientist, discovered that:

'In a fluid at rest in a closed container, a pressure change in one part is transmitted without loss of pressure or fluid to every portion of the fluid and to the walls of the container'.[3]

This became known as Pascal's Principle.

A hydraulic lift, in turn, uses pressurised fluid to move a piston which, subsequently, raises the ramp and vehicle. To lower the ramp, a valve is opened, allowing the fluid to slowly flow back into the reservoir. The weight of the vehicle and gravity do the rest.

Lunati experimented with designs based on the way a barber's chair operated. Whilst lifting was more straightforward, a key safety concern was that, on

---

[3] Encyclopaedia Britannica.

releasing the valve, the car should descend slowly in a controlled manner. Whilst it was easy enough to lower one person in a barber's chair, what about the weight of a steel lift and a hefty vehicle? The mechanic's safety and care of the customer's car were crucial.

On September 1, 1925, Lunati received a patent for his revolutionary lift, the first fully hydraulic automotive lift, and he immediately founded the Automobile Rotary Lift Company. As Lunati's idea caught on, it ushered in a new era in vehicle servicing, transforming the lives of mechanics and making the whole process of servicing cars quicker and more efficient. According to a successor company's website, Lunati's first installation at his garage in Memphis lasted 25 years with an annual operating cost of only 21 cents.

Using his new wealth to build a church

The company did extremely well and would, in time, be called the Dover Elevator Company. Lunati became sufficiently wealthy to return to his principal calling, that of being a pastor. In the 1930s, he financed and built the Assembly Christian Interdenominational Church, taking on the role of pastor there.

He and his wife Lenora Elizabeth (eight years his junior) had several children and, like Peter, they were all committed to their Pentecostalist faith. Lunati died on 19 October 1946, aged just 56; Lenora died many years later in 1984, and many of the family are buried in Elmwood Cemetery, Memphis, where his epitaph reads:

"Inventor, Clergyman,

A friend of Man,

A friend of the Son"

Over the years, designs have changed the structure of lifts. Rather than rotating lifts, it is more common to see two- or four-post lifts, or even scissor-jack lifts, and the rotating action has been abandoned. However, they all utilise the fundamental principles of Pascal, envisioned by Peter Lunati as a means of transforming the quality of life for mechanics.

A Lunati Rotary Lift

Bruce McLaren: So Much More Than a Winning F1 Driver

Many of the heroes featured in this book are, understandably, from the heartlands of the Industrial Revolution, where the automotive industry began – Europe, the US, and, later, Japan. So, what about the southern hemisphere?

Bruce McLaren was a New Zealander who formed part of the antipodean rise in motor sport of the mid-twentieth century. (Bruce's great grandfather was to discover that the family's real surname was 'Howie' and that the McLaren name had been adopted before his ancestors moved from Australia.) Alongside fellow Kiwis Denny Hulme and Chris Amon, and Australians Jack Brabham and Alan Jones, the southern hemisphere earned its share of fearless and tactical Formula 1 drivers. But Bruce McClaren topped them all by also being a gifted car designer, race engineer, and team founder, as well as an elite driver.

Crippling childhood illness

Born in Auckland in 1937, McLaren's parents, Les and Ruth, ran a car service station and workshop in the now-trendy Auckland suburb of Remuera. In his autobiography, McLaren stated:

My younger years were spent learning to broadside around shop corners on two wheels of my tricycle becoming a pest, borrowing mechanics' spanners, etc. just when they needed them, to repair my "racing machine".

Aged just nine, Bruce McLaren was diagnosed with Perthes disease in his left hip. This rare bone condition affects children between the ages of 3 and 10, interrupting blood flow to the femur and weakening this crucial bone, which limits growth and can even cause bone collapse. For McLaren, it resulted in his left leg being shorter than his right leg. As a result, he spent two years in a metal frame and attended The Wilson Home, a residential school for children with disabilities. Meanwhile, his parents – who visited him weekly across the Auckland Bay by ferry – feared that he might never walk again, as his legs were in plaster casts and he was confined to bed. He would have a permanent limp for the rest of his life.

One of his mechanics, Wally Willmott, would later note:

"The effect of Perthes' disease was not a handicap because he had his shoes built up. It wasn't until he put his racing boots on that he would hobble down the road. He would walk on the toe of that foot. It was quite noticeable then, but, otherwise, you were never aware of it. The rumour was that it was actually getting worse. He was very stoic about it. He never mentioned pain or anything like that."[4]

---

[4] https://www.mclaren.com/racing/team/be-brave-beginning-3175496/

The condition may have set him back, but he would never let it stand in the way of his ambitions. He even mastered water skiing on his one good leg.

Talented young racing driver

McLaren progressed to read Engineering at the University of Auckland but dropped out to pursue his interest in motor sport. He was supported by his family, who encouraged him as he enthusiastically steered his Austin Ulster in a figure 8 around the fruit trees in the back garden.

McLaren's first race ended in tragedy when his young team-mate Timmy Mayer was killed. It was a significant moment for Bruce, who recalled:

"To do something well is so worthwhile that to die trying to do it better cannot be foolhardy. It would be a waste of life to do nothing with one's ability, for I feel that life is measured in achievement, not in years alone."

Little did McLaren know that this incident foreshadowed his own fate.

Meanwhile, racing success followed, starting with the 1958 New Zealand Grand Prix. Leaving New Zealand for the UK, in 1959 he joined the Cooper team, alongside Jack Brabham where, aged 22, McLaren won the 1959 USA Grand Prix, the youngest F1 winner at the time. Future Grand Prix wins included the 1960 Argentine, 1962 Monaco and the 1966 Le Mans and 1968 Circuit de Spa-Francorchamps.

Bruce McLaren married Patricia Broad in 1961 and went on to have a daughter, Amanda.

But driving and winning were not enough for Bruce. He was determined that he would use his undoubted design and engineering skills to build his own car and team. He founded McLaren Racing in 1963, starting from humble beginnings in an old brick industrial unit near Heathrow airport.

The inspired designer

A real insight into Bruce's personality occurred in the middle of a race. A fuel filler cap was flapping, and Bruce was initially angry that the door hadn't been properly closed by mechanics. However, the engineer in him realised that the air pressure under the flap was clearly stronger than the airflow above it. Seizing the first opportunity, he grabbed a pair of shears from the pits and busily cut away the bodywork behind the radiator. Immediately, his lap times were faster, giving birth to Team McLaren's iconic 'nostrils' on the nose-cone of the car. Bruce would have been delighted that the first wholly carbon fibre-bodied F1 car would be the 1981 MCL60 McLaren.

With his combination of uncompromising determination, bravery, passion, and talent, Bruce McLaren continues to have a significant impact on the international car racing industry. Today, the team and sports car manufacturing plant are located in state-of-the-art buildings in Woking, Surrey.

Sadly, Bruce died doing what he loved. He crashed at the Goodwood Circuit in England, testing his new McLaren M8D. His earlier epitaph for Timmy Mayer would have been a suitable epitaph for himself. His name lives on, not just in the iconic, bright orange F1 team and the supercar brand, but in the numerous names around his native Auckland, including a retirement home in Howick – ironic for someone who died at just age 32.

Legacy

When you consider the skill set required to be an elite F1 driver (courage, tenacity, daring, extreme competitiveness) and those required of a racing car designer (vision, engineering prowess, close attention to detail, learning from errors and your competitors), these are demanding attributes. On top of that are the different skills needed for starting a business and running a team: entrepreneurialism, financial nous, team management, plus the ability to inspire others and get the best from them. Bruce McLaren displayed all these qualities, never complaining of the physical pain he experienced. Having been bedridden during his childhood, he exalted in and celebrated the freedom of movement and speed in his own design cars. A remarkable life ended too soon.

His widow, Patricia, played a significant role in the team's continuing history, being on the Board of both Bruce McLaren Motor Racing Ltd, and the Bruce McLaren Trust, set up in his name to foster automotive engineering skills. Since Patricia's death in 2016, their only child, Amanda, has continued to support the Trust's aims as a Trustee.[5]

---

[5] https://www.brucemclarentrust.com/

Garrett Morgan: Serial Inventor and Community Activist

The automobile was invented and fostered from its earliest days in Europe and the USA, so it is no surprise that many of its early promoters were Caucasian. Europe itself was predominantly white, as were the earlier days of the USA's northern industrial cities.

Garrett Augustus Morgan was born in 1877 in Paris, Kentucky, of mixed race. He was the seventh of 11 children, born to Elizabeth Reed, who was of Native American and African descent. His father, Sydney, was a former slave, freed in 1863 and himself the son of a Confederate colonel.

This was a truly mixed-race heritage which profoundly influenced his future life and inventions. Aged 14, Morgan moved north to Cincinnati, Ohio and found work as a handyman. Having completed elementary school, he was determined to improve himself, so he paid for a private tutor voluntarily. In 1895, he moved to industrial Cleveland and the following year he married – but the union lasted only two years.

The inventor begins

Morgan's improved skills enabled him to progress to working in a sewing machine factory, which sparked his imagination and vision. He obtained a patent for an improved design and set up his own manufacturing and repair business. Its success allowed him to marry again in 1908, this time to Mary Hasek, a Czech immigrant. However, such was the racism and prejudice at the time that Mary's father was so outraged by the marriage that he successfully applied for his daughter to be excommunicated from the Roman Catholic church into which she was born.

Morgan's inventiveness continued, though. The tailoring shop, run jointly with Mary, encountered problems with some woollen fabrics so Morgan devised a method of straightening the hairs, successfully adapting the technique to uncurl both animal and human hair. The G. A. Morgan Hair Refining Company was born, and its products were sold to African Americans. Its success gave Morgan the financial stability to focus on other inventions.

Encountering prejudice – again

Next came a breathing device or 'safety hood' which he patented in 1914. This allowed wearers to breathe more easily in smoke or gas-filled environments, and it became the prototype for First World War gas masks.

It was used successfully in the 1916 Lake Erie disaster, in which water supply workers were trapped underground in toxic air whilst tunnelling. Hearing of the tunnel's collapse, Morgan and his brother donned their safety hoods, headed underground and saved several lives. For his own personal courage, Morgan was awarded the Medal for Bravery from the city of Erie. The invention also gained first prize at the Second International Exposition of Safety and Sanitation in New York City.

Progress had not been easy, however. Morgan encountered sales resistance in the south because of his colour and had to hire a white actor to demonstrate the product. He was nominated for the Carnegie Prize, although it was rumoured that his ethnicity prevented him from gathering the necessary support for the award.

But what do all these inventions have to do with motoring? By 1922, Morgan had made sufficient money to buy his own car. As one of the first car owners in Cleveland, he witnessed a near-fatal accident at a traffic intersection, and Morgan's next invention is the one for which he became most widely known – the traffic light. Yes, traffic lights already existed, but not with three separate lights, where each single light or combination of lights signalled a different instruction to road users.

Morgan designed a system that was manually operated by a traffic attendant. Moving arms visually stated 'stop' and 'go', and arms that were part-way raised indicated caution or a change of sequence.

Let's consider that. The previous two-light signals really only told you when to stop or go. They did not warn you to get ready to stop or prepare to go, so his invention was quite radical. The three-way light rapidly gained patents in 1923 for the US, UK and Canada. Morgan moved quickly but eventually sold the patent rights for $40,000 to General Electric, which developed an electric version.

A rich legacy

The US Department of Transportation celebrated the centenary of Morgan's traffic signal patent in

November 2023, including a ceremony featuring his granddaughter, Sandra Morgan. Of Morgan's many achievements, biographer Mary Oluonye (see bibliography) said:

"Garrett A Morgan was a gifted problem solver. His inventions provided practical solutions and made significant contributions to public safety issues of the day."

Morgan devoted much of his life to civil rights, becoming an influential community leader in Cleveland. Alas, his health declined, and in 1943, he started to develop glaucoma and gradually lost his sight. His last invention was a self-extinguishing cigarette. A water capsule just below the filter would extinguish the cigarette as it burned down. Morgan died in 1963, when racial matters were at the forefront of US news but before racial equality was established.

Pat Moss Carlsson: Gifted Sportswoman

It is quite some achievement for anyone to excel in a single sport; to do so in two very different sports is exceptional. But that is the story of Pat Moss. Not only was she to shine as a sportswoman but, in doing so, made huge strides in gender equality and female empowerment.

Pat Moss was born in the Home Counties in December 1934 to parents who were immersed in motoring. Her father, Alfred, had had some success as a racing driver, competing in the 1924 Indianapolis 500 race whilst studying dentistry in the USA; her mother Aileen, had success in trials events for several manufacturers, including Singer. Now a successful and wealthy dentist, Alfred and family moved to a farm where Pat's elder brother Stirling (who went on to F1 fame), was to teach the 11-year-old to drive.

Growing up on a farm, Pat Moss became not just enamoured of horses but also a very competent horsewoman. Her successes surpassed simply winning cups and rosettes at gymkhanas; Moss won the 1950 national Horse of the Year Show and progressed to become a member of the British team. At this time, she saw cars merely as a means of towing horse boxes.

However, she was encouraged by Stirling's business manager (who had become her boyfriend) to try out car racing.

Whilst Pat had considerable family support for her equestrian pursuits, this did not extend to her motoring endeavours, which began in 1958 at the age of 18. Being a canny businesswoman, she used her equestrian winnings to buy a Triumph TR2 sports car, although her negotiations with Triumph for sponsorship ultimately came to nothing.

However, motor racing success led a more enlightened BMC (maker of the MG TF, Morris Minor, MG Magnette, Mini Cooper, and Austin-Healey 3000 cars) to recognise her talents. They sponsored her in each of these cars during her early career.

In 1956, she rallied in several British Motor Corporation (BMC) cars: a bulbous Austin A90 (hardly an ideal rally car) in the Monte Carlo Rally, an MGA in the RAC Rally, and an Austin-Healey 3000 on the Liège-Rome-Liège Rally.

Not just a Mini success

Moss's first major international success was the 1958 Tulip Rally in the Netherlands when she was just 27. Her co-driver was Ann Wisdom (collectively they became known as 'Mossie and Wizz'), who proved an ideal teammate, despite her lifelong severe car sickness and being pregnant at the time of the rally.

Perhaps Moss's most celebrated achievement, however, was in the 1962 Tulip Rally in a Mini Cooper. She celebrated the first win for the underestimated Mini against much larger, more powerful cars and was the first woman winner. In total, Pat Moss was to win European Ladies' Champion five times between 1958 and 1965, and the Coupe des Dames a staggering eight times.

In 1960, the Royal Automobile Club recognised her remarkable achievements by presenting her with their Driver of the Year Award. For someone who had fought so hard with heart and soul in a man's world, Pat Moss would have been bemused by the RAC's temporary suspension of its men-only policy in their banquet hall during the award ceremony.

Later achievements

In 1963, Moss was offered a lucrative contract to join Ford, who were keen to promote the rallying potential of their recently introduced Cortina. Named after a chic Italian ski resort, the Cortina went on to phenomenal success in motor sports as well as becoming a family and fleet bestseller. She did join, but was unable to persuade Ford to sponsor her husband, Erik Carlsson, who had enjoyed rallying success with Saab.

A year later, she joined Erik at Saab, rallying its front-wheel-drive two-stroke engine 96, an unusual combination that had proved very successful in its snowy Swedish home territory. After the birth of her daughter, Susan, in 1969, she decreased her rallying commitments. In the meantime, she had found time to write two books, *The Story So Far* and *The Art and Technique of Driving*.

Speeding into the sunset

Pat Moss eventually retired in 1974, at the age of 40, remembered by colleagues and competitors as friendly, generous, and vivacious. However, she continued her interest in horse riding as her daughter Susan developed her own equestrian skills. Moss kept her original green Morris Minor at the back of her garage as a reminder of early wins. She died of cancer at age 73 in 2008, and shortly before her death, she had been caught speeding whilst towing a horsebox, bringing together several aspects of her life.

BMW, as the new manufacturer of the now upper-case MINI, celebrated Moss's achievements. On International Women's Day in 2022, it launched a special edition of 1,000 cars, featuring a bonnet embossed with her winning Monte Carlo Rally Cooper's registration 737 ABL – a fitting tribute to the remarkable achievements of Pat Moss.

Alex Moulton: Small is Beautiful

Whilst the genius for lateral thinking and space-engineering of Sir Alec Issigonis (designer of various cars such as the Morris Minor and the original Mini) is widely known, his inventions would not have been possible without the crucial input of Dr Alex Moulton. Quite simply, without Alex Moulton, the Mini would not have been created.

Alex Moulton was an ingenious engineer who believed that the traditional large-wheeled, diamond-framed bicycle had limitations in comfort and flexibility. To him, building separate bikes for males and females was nonsensical, so he put his considerable engineering skills into small-wheeled designs with rubber suspension. From the grounds of his ancestral home in Bradford-upon-Avon in Wiltshire, he created the Moulton small-wheeled bicycle. It became an icon of the 1960s and has influenced other cycle manufacturers such as Brompton, famous for their folding commuter bikes.

Yet Alex Moulton's background was not in cycling, nor were bikes the main part of the business. Moulton's great-grandfather knew Charles Goodyear of the eponymous American tyre company and he purchased the UK rights to process the vulcanisation of rubber, which made him a fortune, partly by supplying waterproof capes for British soldiers during the Crimean War. With the profits, he bought a Jacobean home, which became central to Alex's life. His own father was a naturalist working in the Far East, so it was not surprising that rubber as a commodity featured in Moulton's work.

The thwarted engineer

After attending public school at nearby Marlborough College, Alex Moulton's Cambridge University education was interrupted by the Second World War. He became an assistant tester at the Bristol Aeroplane Company, and when a colleague was killed in the Bristol Blitz, he was promoted to Junior Technical Assistant. It was a 'reserved occupation', excluding him from frontline military duties.

Whilst frustrated by his restricted duties, Moulton acknowledged the role's potential and remained motivated to learn, marrying theory and practice. Post-war, he resumed his studies at Cambridge, inspired to gain a solid understanding of engineering fundamentals before applying the knowledge in practical applications.

By the late 1950s, the family company was absorbed into Avon Tyres, so Moulton sought a new challenge. He was approached by his good friend Alec Issigonis about an exciting new project: the Morris Mini-Minor.

Moulton maintained in a video interview that Issigonis was dismissive of rubber suspension for anything but lightweight cars, so had used conventional suspension on the Minor. However, for the Mini-Minor he envisaged a small wheel at each corner and a front-wheel drive, transverse engine with the gearbox slung underneath.

Inspired by this concept, Alex established Moulton Developments Ltd to design the Mini's suspension. Conical springs and small wheels were key factors in allowing the Mini to be so compact and nimble. The handling of the Mini Cooper S was legendary, winning an impressive series of Monte Carlo Rallies for Paddy Hopkirk.

From rubber to hydraulic fluid

Over time, suspension design evolved into the Hydrolastic suspension for all Issigonis-designed front-wheel drive British Motor Corporation (BMC) cars in the early and mid-sixties – the 1100, 1300 and the 1800. The implementation interconnected the suspension of all four wheels and stiffened the vehicle as it navigated bends. Hydraulic fluid would be displaced to even out the ride, with the rubber suspension cones having some natural give.

By the early 1970s, Moulton had developed the design into Hydragas, fitted initially to the Allegro, and then to all British Leyland (BL) front-wheel drive cars. This solved some of the problems, such as reducing its bounciness, improving damping, and being simpler to maintain. Yet, despite being fitted to over 15 million British-built vehicles between 1959 and 2000, it did not prevent large numbers of the British motoring public from falling out of love with the overall build quality of BMC products. The troubles and later demise of the parent company, which variously called itself BMC, BMH (British Motor Holdings), BL and ultimately, Rover, were not of Moulton's making.

Bouncing back to rubber

Moulton's focus returned in 1983 to his cycle, cited for its "*sparse beauty*" by Norman Foster, the famous architect. Foster felt that it represented "*The greatest work of 20th-century British design*" and, as a 'mini-bike', was "*synonymous with the Mini and the mini-skirt.*"[6]

Alex Moulton at home

For his engineering innovations, Moulton was awarded the CBE, several honorary doctorates, and was widely recognised by the engineering profession for his distinguished and independent-minded service. His alumnus profile for Cambridge University refers to him

[6] Tribute by Foster in *The Architect's Journal.* 11 December 2012.

as "*idiosyncratic, intensely intelligent and strongly driven*". Although he sold his company to Raleigh during a time of financial difficulty, he later bought back the patents.

The ethical businessman

Moulton lived quietly in Wiltshire, suggesting that he had remained unmarried due to his devotion to both engineering and the Jacobean family home – "The Hall" – in Bradford-upon-Avon. Regarded by some as eccentric, he had a strict moral code for business. Whilst recognising the need to make a profit, he believed that the social good should take precedence over mere financial gain. This principle is reflected in the legacy of his charitable trust. It serves both to promote the cause of engineering and education, as well as the preservation of the ancestral home.

Moulton remained active till his final years, both hiking and kayaking into his 80s and riding his beloved Moulton bike into his 90s. He died, aged 92, in 2012, but the Moulton Bicycle Company continues today with a fiercely loyal customer base.

Ben Nevis: Versus Henry Alexander Jr.

OK, a bit of a cheat. Ben Nevis is not a person, of course, but the highest peak in the UK, located in the Grampian Mountains near Fort William in Scotland. At 1345 metres (4,413 feet), it has always been a challenge to climb on foot – but by car?

In 1911, Henry Alexander became the first Ford dealer in Scotland, when he imported the Ford Model T car from the United States. Launched three years earlier, it was the car that built Henry Ford's reputation for producing a model that sold globally and confirmed his standing as the master of the moving production line. What, wondered Alexander, would be a suitable publicity stunt to promote the brand, the car and his Edinburgh dealership? In particular, he wanted to promote the belief that mass-produced cars were just as reliable and durable as those from brands that were still hand-built and which sold for a substantially higher price.

So, in 1911, a 20 hp, four-seat Model T Tourer (in black, of course) was selected as the ideal model. An open-topped Tourer did not have a heavy roof or side windows to dismantle or to make the car top-heavy on its treacherous path, but this was the only concession to weight. The driver would be Mr Alexander's own son, Henry Jr., who was dragooned into the role. Rumour has it that if he had not agreed, his allowance would have been stopped; his first task was to drive the car from Edinburgh to Fort William (a distance of 146 miles).

Impeccable logistical planning

Of course, getting a car up a mountain doesn't just happen, even in the early summer time when the very worst of the snow and ice has melted. Taking on this mighty adversary meant ten gruelling days of reconnaissance work to devise the most appropriate ascent. Then the team needed an array of planks and ropes shipped up by Highland ponies to enable the car to traverse gullies and streams. And, if these devices didn't work, a supply of dynamite to blast a route through intractable obstacles was at hand! This demonstrates how the expedition was of its time, and would be environmentally unacceptable today.

Setting off from nearby Torlundy, the team followed a zig-zag route towards the summit. It was to take three days to drive just halfway up. No smooth tarmac or gravel path here – the route was across sharp-edged rocks, ice- and snow-fields, treacherous scree fields, gullies and ravines.

And, of course, there was also the need for a large support team to push the car and to haul it out of muddy, boggy patches onto harder terrain. At the end of each day, the car was left where it had reached, covered by a tarpaulin, and Henry Jr made his way on foot back to a Fort William hotel.

They completed the climb on the 18th of May, and a posse of newspaper photographers and film-makers, complete with heavy wooden tripods, was there to record the extraordinary feat.

Heroic drive captured on film

A slow and gruelling five-day ascent was to be followed by a hair-raising and rapid descent. A film of the descent was rediscovered in 2015 and is now available to watch, free, as part of the British Film Institute's archive.[7] At one point, to our present-day horror, a precious peat-bank is dynamited, scattering debris everywhere.

The malleable suspension is seen working overtime as the car bounces across the rocks on its skinny wheels and tyres. What a bone-shaking, jarring ride it must have been for young Henry.

What is fascinating about the film – apart from the route, the manhandling of the vehicle, and the treacherous conditions – are the clothes worn by Henry Jr.: a tweed 'Plus-4' suit, together with a shirt and tie, and a hat. At times, you'll see that he is even gloveless. These days, no mountaineer, even an amateur, would go without specifically-designed clothing – waterproof, moisture-wicking and lightweight. How heavy, damp and clinging would that tweed outfit have felt? You can just about work out some 'chains' on the rear wheels but, otherwise, the car is a standard production model.

Given that this expedition was essentially a publicity stunt, the only advertising signage visible was the extra-large Ford lettering. Valuable opportunities missed, one would think.

---

[7] https://player.bfi.org.uk/free/film/watch-motoring-over-ben-nevis-1911-online

Rapturous welcome for the adventurer

On his arrival in Fort William, Henry Jr. was given a hero's welcome. The triumphant driver and his car, now bedecked with the Scottish Lion Rampant and the US Stars and Stripes, made its slow path through streets thronged with flag-waving well-wishers. A bagpipe and drum military band added to the occasion. Henry checked and adjusted the brakes and then drove the car back to Edinburgh.

Was that it? No.

Having inherited the dealership from his father, Henry Jr. returned to Ben Nevis in September 1928, undaunted by his earlier escapade. This time, he made a repeat ascent in a recently-launched Ford Model A Tourer, taking just nine and a half hours, and two hours the following day to descend! The Model A heralded a new era in motoring as, unlike its predecessor, it had four-wheel drum brakes, hydraulic shock absorbers and conventional foot pedals (the Model T was infamous for having them 'back to front'). Imagine descending Ben Nevis with brakes on only two wheels!

Henry's inspirational legacy

More recently, in 2011, to commemorate the centenary of Henry's feat, a team of volunteers sought to recreate the spirit of the original journey. Prevented by modern environmental laws from actually driving a car up Ben Nevis, they devised an alternative – dismantling a replica Model T into 77 pieces. The 60 volunteers in this tribute each carried the car's components to the summit by hand. Fighting strong winds, hail, and snow, at the summit they reassembled the replica and took a commemorative photograph, before dismantling it and carrying it back down.

On the 18th of May 2018, a bronze statue of the original car (registration S1871), with Henry Jr., resplendent in his tweed Plus-4 suit and tie, was unveiled in Fort William's Cameron Square. He had met his adversary head-on twice, and over the next century, inspired others to do so.

Ransom E. Olds: The Founder of Mass Production

Who was the father of the US automobile industry? Many people would grant Henry Ford this accolade. Or perhaps Henry Leland, founder of Cadillac? Neither is correct. Many historians would instead identify Ransom Eli Olds, founder of the Olds Motor Vehicle Company.

Born in Ohio in 1864 into a family that ran a machine shop, the young Ransom was, from the outset, fascinated with all sorts of transportation engineering.

Forever tinkering

In 1880, the family moved to Lansing, Michigan, and Olds was to be instrumental in making the town a hub of the automobile industry.

He loved tinkering with every sort of steam and petrol engine design, and his early invention of a steam engine with a gas burner for a boat was later adapted for use in a car. By 1897, he had registered the Olds Motor Vehicle Company, in association with investor Edward Sparrow, whose fortune came from timber.

Throughout life, no matter how gifted Olds was as an engineer, his skills did not always extend to working with others, Sparrow included. After a falling out between them over whether the company should focus on small or large cars, the company was sold to Samuel Smith in 1899, with Olds staying on in the role of Vice-President and General Manager. Smith relocated production 90 miles to Detroit, establishing the first permanent automobile factory in what would become known as 'Motor City'. But tense relationships continued, not least because Olds wanted Oldsmobile, as it was now called, to stay in Lansing.

Ahead of the Curve

Olds continued experimenting, this time with his most famous innovation – the stationary assembly line. However, success was short-lived, as the Detroit factory burned down the very same year it opened, 1901.

Olds relocated back to Lansing, taking with him the sole survivor of the fire, a prototype of his Curved Dash model. This car was to prove extremely popular, partly because of its visual similarity to a horse-drawn buggy, thus easing the transition from horse power to motor power for many buyers. Such was his confidence in the car, Olds pre-sold 300 before production started. The Curved Dash Olds became the top-selling car of its era in the USA, with total sales of 19,000 by 1905, and even became famous in popular culture with the hit song '*In My Merry Oldsmobile*'.

An Oldsmobile Curved Dash

Production disagreements arose again, and Olds left in 1904. Using his initials, he formed the R.E. Olds Motor Car Company. Later, this was changed to the REO Motor Car Company to avoid a lawsuit with Oldsmobile. REO rapidly became more successful than the original company, particularly with the trucks it produced during the First World War. The legendary 1915 Speed Wagon (sometimes called Reo Speedwagon) reached sales of 125,000 by 1925.

Meanwhile, Oldsmobile had been sold in 1908 to the newly formed General Motors (GM) as one of its first two operating divisions. In time, it became part of the GM 'ladder of success' hierarchy, occupying the middle ground between Chevrolet, Pontiac, then Oldsmobile, Buick and top brand, Cadillac. In 1936, Oldsmobile, now recognised as the experimental division of GM, chalked up its one millionth sale. This was a fitting tribute to Olds's earlier achievements, even though he was no longer involved in the brand.

A quirky magnate

Ransom Olds moved into a magnificent Queen Anne-style mansion he had built on the banks of the Grand River in Lansing. It had many luxurious fittings, including a garage turntable to save him from reversing his car. There may have been logic to this feature, but his wealth also revealed some eccentricities in his personality. Determined that his wife would be younger than him, he had married Metta Ursula Woodward in June 1889. Metta was indeed younger by three days.

An entry in his diary reportedly noted that Lansing manufacturers should not employ those who were not regular church-goers (so much for diversity). Likewise, at REO, Olds used spies to identify workers who smoked on the job or outside the factory gates, then fired the smokers. Goodness knows what Ransom Olds would have made of the rock band that named themselves after one of his most successful creations, the REO Speedwagon.

Despite these oddities, Olds is regarded as a hugely influential figure in automobile heritage. Having retired in 1936 (the same year that REO ended car production to concentrate solely on trucks), Ransom E. Olds died in Lansing, Michigan, in 1950, aged 86. He had seen significant changes to the industry. For some years, the Curved Dash runabout reigned supreme, and the static production line would be adapted successfully by Henry Ford into a moving line. This system is now the norm universally, albeit with robots doing much of the work. Olds remains the only US motoring pioneer to have built vehicles using a variety of power sources – steam, petrol, and diesel.

Gerald Palmer: Style That Hit The Mark

Gerald Palmer designed some of the mid-twentieth century's most attractive and desirable British cars. Each of them deserves a place in a Concours d'Elegance procession.

Born in 1911, Gerald was raised in what was then Rhodesia. From his railway engineer father, he inherited an old Model T Ford, which he stripped down to create a sports car. He came to the UK in 1927, having gained an apprenticeship with truck maker Scammell in Watford, which was renowned for its production of heavy-duty and military vehicles. He also studied engineering at the prestigious Regent Street Polytechnic. On the side, inspired by the 'special' he'd created in Rhodesia, he designed a little sports car, the Deroy, named after a tin mine owned by his father in Mozambique.

Palmer was sufficiently confident to demonstrate it in Abingdon to MG's founder, Cecil Kimber. Although they did not adopt it, MG saw promise in the sporty engineering and recommended Gerald for a job at Morris Motors in Cowley, Oxford. At the age of 27, he joined the MG design office in 1938.

Then, as with several other people featured in this book, the outbreak of a war diverted Gerald from his allotted task of creating the MG Y-Type. Instead, he worked on Tiger Moth planes and repairing Spitfires. During this period, the boss of Morris, Lord Nuffield, instructed Gerald to improve the design of a portable 'Oxford Vaporiser', a key aid in military hospitals for delivering ether anaesthesia.

Go north, young man

In 1941, Palmer saw a job advertisement in The Automotive Engineer for the position of Chief Designer at an unspecified company. It turned out to be Jowett in Bradford, which had a reputation for building unexciting but reliable and affordable cars, and in particular, vans. The brief was to create a car for the post-war world.

Having been initially intrigued by the role, Palmer declined the job offer when he discovered it was for Jowett, far away from the traditional heartlands of the British motor industry. He also felt conflicted. He was working on war-related designs – was this really the time to fantasise about future cars? Jowett's MD, Charles Calcott-Reilly, would not take no for an answer, however, and persuaded him that he would be creating a vision of well-deserved peacetime motoring. He pursued Palmer until he agreed in 1942 to the role for £500 a year. This was a considerable rise from the £325 he was earning at Morris.

A huge challenge and a unique achievement

Gerald was given a free hand to envision what he thought the post-war motorist would value. He had the rare gift of being able to design both the bodywork and the oily bits and the result was the Javelin. Like its namesake, it had an aerodynamic shape, and Gerald designed every part of the car, except for the gearbox and back axle. His work included the body styling, the flat-four aluminium engine, the transmission, chassis and suspension. The Javelin's tear-drop, sleek lines could accommodate six people in considerable comfort and looked spectacular. It could accelerate effortlessly and cruise at 80mph.

The bodies were built by sub-contractors Briggs in Doncaster (where they also built the Ford Anglia bodies) and transported to the Bradford assembly line. Briggs met their contract, resulting in a far greater number of bodies being supplied and stockpiled than the number of Javelin orders received. The car also proved to have some reliability issues, but Jowett had inadequate resources to remedy these weaknesses at an early stage. Nevertheless, Palmer himself co-drove a Javelin to a Class win in the 1949 Monte Carlo Rally, demonstrating the car's potential. Alas, that potential was not realised; lacking finance, Jowett would enter voluntary liquidation in 1954.

A 1953 Jowett Javelin

A clean sweep of sensational designs

Always eager to take on a challenge, Gerald was attracted back to the Morris organisation later in 1949. It was keen to inject some new life into its ageing MG, Riley and Wolseley brands. He was appointed to design the MG Magnette, the Wolseley 4/44, the Riley Pathfinder, and its sibling, the Wolseley 6/90. The big six-cylinder Wolseley, like many of the brand's previous models, became a stalwart of the police forces, frequently featuring in films and TV crime series of the 50s and 60s. All the new models marked a significant advance from his pre-war Y-Type, whose debut had been delayed until 1947.

By 1952, Morris and its subsidiaries had merged with Austin to form the British Motor Corporation (BMC). Palmer's success led him to become Chief Designer.

However, it was not a happy time for him, a calm man, amidst the tumultuous company politicking. Before long, BMC's mercurial boss, Leonard Lord, fired him, and it was rumoured that he wanted to replace the gentle, courteous designer with the more flamboyant Alec Issigonis, who, having designed the Morris Minor, would go on to inspire many innovative cars for BMC (see Alex Moulton p119).

For the final part of his career, Gerald moved in 1955 to Vauxhall, General Motors' UK subsidiary. Here, he became Assistant Chief Engineer – Passenger Cars, a managerial rather than a creative role. He oversaw the introduction of the FB Victor, the slab-sided HA Viva and the stunningly elegant follow-on HB Series Viva models of the 1960s, before retiring in 1972.

A busy and focused retirement

In retirement, this self-deprecating and quiet man was always surprised at the level of interest and fondness shown for the cars he had created. He continued his work on medical aids, designing the Oxford Hoist to assist disabled patients in and out of bed. Versions of which are still in widespread use today, providing a safe and secure means of movement for patients and alleviating back strain for healthcare staff.

In his spare time, Palmer's methodical nature and pride in end-results helped him restore both a Type 44 Bugatti and – over a dedicated 20-year period and from tea-chests of parts – a prized racing Mercedes, winner of the 1924 Targa Florio.

Gerald had married Diana in 1939, had one daughter and continued to live in the Oxford house he had designed himself. In 1998, thoughtful and modest to the last, he collaborated on the writing of his own autobiography, which was published a year before his death in 1999, at the age of 88.

Armand Peugeot:
Peppered with Praise

Have you ever been in a smart restaurant and noticed the pepper mills at your table? Did they have a little lion emblem? If so, they were made by Peugeot, who were to later extend their expertise from the gears of pepper, salt and coffee mills to other uses.

During the eighteenth century, Jean-Pierre Peugeot (born 1734), descended from Lutherans in Switzerland, started the industrial company that would become one of France's largest conglomerates. The Peugeot company was founded in 1810 when Jean-Pierre's sons, Jean-Pierre II and Jean-Frédéric, adapted their flour mill in Hérimoncourt, eastern France, to become a steel mill.

Granted a patent for a new method of steel cold-rolling in 1819, the company began to manufacture a variety of tools, clock and watch mechanisms, as well as domestic products such as irons, sewing machines, and steel hoops for ladies' garments.

They also owned a beech forest, which was ideal for crafting the handles of many of their products. By 1840, they had made their first coffee mill, patenting the milling system. Its success meant that they followed it with the pepper mill, and the success of their products propelled them not only to the forefront of engineering but also made them very rich.

Fascination with engineering

By 1851, a new company, Peugeot Frères (founded by Jean-Pierre II's sons, Jules and Émile) had been established. Into this wealthy family, Armand was born in 1849, and he became absorbed with engineering at a young age and went off to Paris to study at the prestigious engineering school, École Centrale. He was in good company, as the university had attracted other notable engineering alumni, including Panhard, Levassor, Michelin, Gustave Eiffel, and Louis Blériot.

Graduating from here, Armand decided to travel across the English Channel to Britain, which was home to a rapidly expanding cycle-building industry. Seeing the enormous growth of this industry, Armand subsequently returned to France, where he and his cousin Eugène (born 1844) joined the family steel industry. Both cousins encouraged the Peugeot business to diversify away from domestic tools into cycle building, which it started to do in 1882. Three types of cycle were offered: the large two-seater (at a low price but with two or three gears) and a single or two-seater tricycle.

The young visionary

The company's expertise in manufacturing reliable and smooth gearing provided a growing business opportunity in the emerging industrial revolution across France. The nation was witnessing the growth of all sorts of wheeled transport, including cars. Armand Peugeot was fascinated by cars; he was a visionary and was bold with his initiatives. By 1891, Peugeot had become an established brand in France and beyond.

Armand was convinced of the success of their joint endeavours and the potential of the petrol-powered Type 2 Quadricycle, powered by a Daimler engine. Cousin Eugène, however, was reticent about investing huge sums of money into automobile manufacture, and as a result of a family rift, the cousins split the business in two in 1896. Armand's company was called *La Société Anonyme des Automobiles Peugeot* and would concentrate on building cars in the town of Audincourt, eastern France. It was to be the world's first factory dedicated to building cars. Legally, his company was forbidden to make tools, build two-wheeled vehicles (bicycles), tricycles or the newly fashionable quadricycles. Meanwhile, the legal terms of the separation meant that Eugène's *Les Fils de Peugeot Frères* was prevented from building cars but could build other products.

Armand's personal life was also busy. He had married Sophie in 1872, and they went on to have five children.

However, he was devastated by losing his only son and male heir, Raymond, in 1896. By 1910, the two cousins' companies had again merged. It became France's largest vehicle manufacturer by 1913, the year of his retirement, producing 10,000 cars a year.

Social impact of the Peugeot family

In another parallel with fellow Lutheran engineer Rudolf Diesel, the Peugeot company also gained recognition for its commitment to enhancing the lives of its workers and providing social benefits. For example, it instituted a ten-hour working day, a mutual assistance society for employees, low-cost employee housing, professional training and employee pensions, which, from 1811, included widows' pensions. These were ground-breaking improvements in social conditions by an employer.

Armand died in 1915, but his vision lives on. His company became a major player in Groupe PSA and subsequently, the Stellantis conglomerate. He was accepted into the Automotive Hall of Fame in 1999.

Armand's vision and energy led to Peugeot becoming an international brand, and Peugeot remains one of the world's few manufacturers producing such a breadth of transportation modes, including bicycles, mopeds, scooters, cars, vans, minibuses and light trucks. It continues to produce electric drills and those pepper, salt and coffee mills, whose parts are considered impossible to wear out.

Armand Peugeot

Dorothée Pullinger: Entrepreneuse Extraordinaire

Have you ever found a car's controls and layout unsuited to your body shape and size? Difficult to reach pedals? Too much of a stretch for certain controls? Can't see clearly where the bonnet ends? Step forward Dorothée Aurélie Marianne Pullinger. Designing a car was not her only engineering creation or entrepreneurial activity – but was perhaps her most significant.

Born in Normandy, France, in 1894 to an engineer father, Thomas, Dorothée was schooled initially in Loughborough, England. She then moved to Scotland in 1902, where her father had been appointed Managing Director of the Arrol-Johnston car company in Paisley. Despite her clear ability to progress to university, her family expected her, as the eldest child, to stay at home and help run the family home of 11 children. But by age 16, Dorothée's heart was set on becoming an engineer and in 1910, she persuaded her father to employ her as a Junior in the Arrol-Johnston drawing office. Her artistic ability as a child is clear to see in the drawings she made of the family farm (see bibliography).

From rejection to success

Applying to join the Institution of Automobile Engineers in 1914, she was rejected on the grounds that "*the word person means a man and not a woman*". The 20-year-old's abilities were swiftly recognised, though, as with the outbreak of the First World War, she became the Lady Superintendent of the 7,000 women workers at the Barrow-in-Furness plant of Vickers munitions. Here, her bilingual skills in dealing with many French and Belgian war refugee workers came to the fore, as well as her engineering prowess.

Manufacturing practice rooted in belief in women

At the war's end, Dorothée became a founding Member of the Women's Engineering Society, and by 1920, aged just 26, she was awarded an MBE for her war work. This was a stunning achievement by any measure!

During the war, many women had held skilled, technical jobs in order to release men into military roles. Some had also learnt to drive. Seizing this potential market growth, Dorothée persuaded her father to set up a subsidiary of Arrol-Johnston, producing a car that was specially designed for women. She became the Director of Galloway Engineering Company in Tongland, Kirkcudbright, with a predominantly female workforce. Factory facilities included a swimming pool, a rooftop tennis court, a hockey team and a piano room. Apprenticeships were reduced in length from five years to three, as Dorothée believed that women were better attendees and quicker learners than young men.

The Galloway 1528cc, 4-cylinder car (based on redesigned Fiat 501 origins) was promoted in *Light Car and Cyclecar* publication in 1921 as "*a car built by ladies, for those of their own sex*". Some of Dorothée's modifications included: a lighter and smaller body yet more storage space, a raised and more adjustable seat to give a clearer view of the road, a lowered dashboard, a smaller steering wheel, a more conveniently-situated handbrake and gear lever (to facilitate stepping in and out whilst wearing long skirts) and a rear-view mirror. Redesigned foot pedals meant less of a stretch for smaller feet, and from 1926, four-wheel brakes enhanced the handling. A 1927 model featured regularly in the *Dr Finlay's Casebook* TV series.

By 1923, production had moved to Heathhall, a former aircraft factory in Dumfries and the factory was renamed Galloway Motors Ltd. 4,000 examples were produced until the end of the decade, during the latter years sporting an Arrol-Johnston badge. However, compared with production-line built Austin and Morris models, the hand-built cars were expensive, and production of all Arrol-Johnstons ceased in 1928.

Honours continued to be bestowed on Dorothée, who was now the first female member of the Institution of Automobile Engineers. By this time, she had moved to England, where she became the southern England sales representative for Galloway. And then, heading in a completely different direction, she founded a new business – White Service Laundries in Croydon. With its own power station and arterial well, the laundry used innovative US-steam laundry machines and grew the business to an empire of 17 outlets.

National recognition

When war broke out again, Dorothée's skills and experience were snapped up by her once-rival car manufacturer, Lord Nuffield of Morris Motors. He commissioned her to organise women recruits in the many munitions factories which he had set up for the war effort. Her skills and leadership qualities in running 13 factories were such that she became the sole female member of the Ministry of Production's industrial panel.

Post-war, Dorothée moved with her husband and two children to Guernsey. She had correctly spotted the growing tourist potential of Guernsey and the rise in the number of hotels and guesthouses. So, extending her entrepreneurial skills, she established Normandie Laundries. Still with a clear knack for managing women employees and harnessing their goodwill, Dorothée always ensured that the workers' Christmas bonus was a piece of meat, sometimes even the luxury of duck. In an era of food shortages and rationing, she reasoned that this gift would be appreciated by the whole family rather than risking the workers' husbands squandering a cash bonus in the pub. Today, the business continues to be run by the family, although it is also a dry cleaning business. Dying at the age of 92 in 1986, Dorothée remains the only woman to have designed and engineered the production of a car with female drivers in mind.

A Galloway 10.20

Billy Rootes: The Tycoon Who Built a Conglomerate But Let One Brand Slip Away

William (or Billy) Rootes was one of the most successful manufacturers of well-known British car brands. He built his two-pronged empire from humble beginnings to become one of the UK's largest dealers and manufacturers of the twentieth century.

Born in 1894 to William Sr., Billy spent his childhood watching his father slowly build his cycling and motorcycling sales and repair shop in Goudhurst, Kent. William Sr. had scraped together enough savings to open his repair shop and optimistically foresaw the rapid rise of the automobile business. He wanted to be part of it, telling the boys, "*There's a future in motor cars*". However, as a teenager, Billy had no desire to join his father's business and left school in 1909 to join Singer Motors in Coventry as an apprentice. Earning a penny an hour, little did he know then that he would, in time, buy the company.

Brothers in arms

After his apprenticeship, Billy returned home to join his father's business, now diversified into a motor dealership. By 1913, it had opened a branch in

Maidstone, which Billy was appointed to manage. The First World War intervened, and Billy served in the Royal Naval Volunteer Reserve. His demobilisation instructions were to establish a plant in Maidstone where aero engines could be repaired instead of being scrapped. This responsibility and experience set the scene for the future.

By 1920, Billy had persuaded younger brother Reginald to relinquish his civil service career in the Admiralty and join him in the motor trade. The brothers became Joint Managing Directors of Rootes Motors, distributors for a variety of marques. They grew to become the UK's largest distributors as they cannily bought dealerships across England. Before long, further expansion saw the brothers create a new central London HQ at Devonshire House in Piccadilly, reflecting their premier position in the motor trade.

The company visionary

Billy was always the company visionary. He had a knack for marketing, which served him well. However, not content with Rootes Motors merely selling and servicing cars, Billy now wanted to actually manufacture them. With a keen eye for a bargain, in 1927, he snapped up ailing manufacturers Humber and Hillman with their ageing model range. Commer Trucks followed in 1935, then Sunbeam and Karrier.

Their first new Hillman did not sell well, but its follow-up, the Minx, was an immediate success, setting the standard of being an inexpensive and reliable small family car. Billy was directly involved in the Minx's development, completing all the overseas testing himself. Their garage in Maidstone was built in 1938 as a 'modern model garage' and is now a Grade II listed Art Deco building.

Billy's vision was to differentiate the brands. Commer was the principal truck brand for the commercial market; Karrier became the division specialising in local council vehicles (like dustcarts and street sweepers), even though they shared the same cabs and some mechanical parts.

The car divisions distinguished themselves more subtly. Whilst Billy saw tremendous advantages in cost savings and flexibility by sharing engines, chassis and other components, his instinct was to target different market segments. Hillman was the main brand, aimed at middle-class buyers seeking no-nonsense reliability and value-for-money. Sunbeams were sporty, and Humber represented luxury. During the 1930s, each brand retained its own look even while sharing some parts.

By 1937, the Rootes Group had become a conglomerate of eight manufacturers, seven distributors, and a number of finance and property companies. Manufacturing across the market spectrum, it employed 10,000 people and was rightly considered a jewel of British business, with an insightful and astute leader.

As with other manufacturers, the arrival of the Second World War stifled domestic car production, and the focus became military vehicles. The 'Shadow Factories' scheme was a government initiative to enable manufacturers to transfer their skills in assembly work and production line techniques from cars to building military aircraft. It was a huge success for Rootes, both as a company and for Billy's personal skill set. He had the experience and vision to see what was needed; the ability to instil high standards in a motivated workforce and the government connections to get things done. Rootes produced one in seven of the UK's bombers, 30% of Scout cars and an incredible 50,000 aero engines. As a result, in 1942, Billy was awarded a knighthood (now being known as Sir William), with brother Reggie gaining one in 1946.

William drops a clanger

During this immediate post-war era, though, Sir William Rootes, made a dreadful error. As the entry on Ivan Hirst (p60) explains, he failed to see the potential in the Wolfsburg plant of the Volkswagen Beetle. During its extensive lifetime, the Beetle went on to become a global bestseller.

Nevertheless, business remained good and Sir William retained his knack for marketing and for spotting other likely investment opportunities. In 1955, Rootes bought his old apprenticeship provider, Singer Motors, which was suffering from outmoded, uncompetitive designs. He swiftly brought it into the Rootes hierarchy, placing it one brand higher than Hillman. Clothed in their Rootes Audax body, the new Minx and upmarket variations were well-received, setting the template for all future Rootes cars. Hillman and Singer versions shared not just the same engine and components but also the same body panels. The Sunbeam Rapier two-door coupe sported twin carburettors and won the 1958 RAC Rally. Later cars followed a similar body panel sharing approach.

Good and bad news

In 1959, two key things happened that affected Sir William. The good news was that he was created a Baron, becoming Lord Rootes of Ramsbury in Wiltshire. The bad news was the launch of the Mini by BMC, from which the Rootes Group never recovered.

Their own planned competitor was the small, rear-engined Hillman Imp. Government funding rules meant that the Imp factory had to be in an area of economic deprivation – Linwood, Scotland. Far from Rootes' Midlands factories, it was staffed by former shipbuilders, unused to the greater engineering tolerances of automobile manufacture. Launched in 1963 before all the technical problems had been resolved, the Imp proved Lord Rootes' second misjudgement with a rear-engined car. It could never compete technically or in manufacturing terms with the Mini – components had to be shipped back and forth between Linwood and the Midlands for different stages of processing.

Financial and workforce trouble

By the early 1960s, the company had little cash to invest, and the poor labour relations endemic across the whole UK motor industry were costing it dear. Despite the introduction of the Minx-replacement Arrow series from 1966, the Rootes Group was in financial difficulty. A genuine Ford Cortina rival, the Hillman Hunter and derivatives could not compete. Without foreign investment, Lord Rootes' skill for marketing was facing insurmountable challenges. Putting a brave face on matters, Rootes accepted a takeover by the US's Chrysler which, after a few years, sold out their European operations to Peugeot.

So, a motoring hero? Yes, despite two poor decisions, Billy Rootes demonstrated impeccable planning and production capability in wartime and great marketing skill in peacetime. His ability saw him appointed to oversee the reconstruction of blitz-ravaged Coventry, home to many of his factories and to establish the University of Warwick. He died in 1964 before he could become its first Chancellor.

Percy Shaw: One for The Road

Having a pub named after you is an aspiration for some people. Certainly, it's not a bad epitaph. Nell Gwyn, Charlie Chaplin, John Fielding VC (of the Boer War's Rorke's Drift fame), and Sir Frank Whittle (jet engine designer) are among those who have achieved this accolade. So, if you visit *The Percy Shaw* in Halifax, you might wonder after whom it is named. Indeed, a pub is integral to this story.

Halifax resident Percy Shaw is one of the great pioneers of safe motoring, yet his name is not widely known today. Born in 1890, the fourth child of a dye-works labourer father, Shaw left school at 13 to work in a local cloth mill. When the works closed, father and son set up a business adjoining their house, making tools. Here they gained a reputation for turning their skilful hands to all sorts of manufacturing, including shell noses and cartridge cases in the First World War.

Illuminating the way home

On the death of his parents, Shaw progressed to setting up a tarmac-laying business. Driving home from his customary pub one foggy evening, he caught sight of a cat at the roadside. In fact, all he could see was its eyes, piercing the darkness and the mist. What if, he thought, there was a series of cats' eyes spaced out along the centre line of the road to illuminate the way home? It was Shaw's Eureka moment.

A switched-on Yorkshire inventor, Shaw set to experimenting. But his best bet was just to copycat. He proceeded to sheath an iron shoe in rubber, in which he implanted two reflectors cut like diamonds to catch light from a variety of angles. Being a tarmac layer, it is rumoured that he used this skill to dig up road sections overnight, lay his road studs, drive past numerous times to see how the headlights reflected, reinstate the road, then set off home to further refine his design. By 1934, he had patented a design and, encouraged by the emphasis on road safety in that year's Road Traffic Act, (see Leslie Hore Belisha, p70), Shaw set up Reflecting Roadstuds Ltd. to produce the Catseye (no apostrophe). The name is registered, so no competitor can use it, and his Halifax company still trades today.

Ingenious design

The real brilliance of the road stud's design lies not just in the bright reflection of light but in its self-cleaning ability. The rubber mount is suspended in a bracket, so that every time a vehicle runs over a Catseye, a squirt of residual rainwater in the iron casing cleans the reflectors. They don't need any special maintenance – just let nature keep them sparkling.

At first, sales were excruciatingly slow, but were boosted by the increasing emphasis on road safety. The wartime blackout was to prove beneficial as Shaw was called to Whitehall to explain his invention. He achieved sufficient government funding to produce 40,000 of his reflecting studs. However, Japan's entry into the war and invasion of Malaya slashed the supply of rubber dramatically. Experiments with scrap rubber failed to work properly – apart from recycling the crepe soles of shoes and boots. Once the war was over, however, Reflecting Roadstuds' production bounced back.

Twenty years later, in 1965, Shaw was awarded the OBE for services to export, and today, the company produces a million items a year.

Spartan pleasures

Percy Shaw led an almost austere life. Despite his wealth – allegedly becoming a multi-millionaire – he continued to live in the very same Halifax home (Boothtown Mansion, right next to his factory) that his parents had moved into when he was just two years old. He stayed there right up until his death in 1976, aged 86. Well-known TV journalist Alan Whicker made a memorable documentary in 1968, which showed that, despite his wealth, Shaw lived a simple bachelor's life. His home had no carpets or curtains because "*they collected dust*" and there was hardly any furniture – except for a TV set in each of four rooms. What was striking in these pre-remote-control days was that each set was left permanently on and tuned to a different station. Did the shining white dot in the centre of the screen, when transmission ended, remind him of his own invention?

Percy Shaw (left) with Alan Whicker

Yet, Shaw did have some pleasures – the pub, friends' company, golf, as well as TV. His prized possession was tucked away in his garage, a Rolls-Royce Phantom V limousine. It was his one real luxury. Sporting the personal registration plate PS 1274, such a car would usually have been fitted by the manufacturers with a glass division between the chauffeur and passengers. But not for Percy. Given his delight in driving the limousine, Percy specified that the glass division should not be fitted, so that he could maintain chatting easily with the friends he drove to his local golf club. That was not the only unusual aspect of owning such a prestigious car. Percy was remembered in the local newspaper for regularly buying tripe in the town market and, so legend had it, he would sometimes eat it with his bare fingers in the rear seats. How he kept his greasy fingers off the luxurious leather interior is unknown!

The pub bearing his name was sold on in January 2024 by Wetherspoons to a small, independent local brewery, who has committed to keeping its name and legacy. Whilst Percy's life was certainly eccentric, his contribution to road safety was huge, through an invention we all take for granted.

Alfred P. Sloan: The Greatest US Businessman?

Was Alfred P. Sloan a titan of '*The American Dream*' or someone with little sense of what the American business psychologist, Douglas McGregor, called '*The human side of enterprise*'?

Let's start at the beginning.

Alfred Pritchard Sloan was born, the first of five children, in New Haven, Connecticut in 1875. His father was a successful coffee merchant and an investor in a number of companies, including the Hyatt Roller company.

When the family moved to Brooklyn, New York, Alfred attended local schools and was fascinated by the engineering discoveries of his childhood. He did well in his studies and, aged just 17, progressed to Massachusetts Institute of Technology (MIT), graduating in electrical engineering at 20.

His father secured him a draughtsman's job at Hyatt Roller, which made roller bearings for vehicle axles and transmissions, including Olds. Hyatt had just won a prestigious contract with the upmarket manufacturer, Cadillac, but all was not well. Soon, Sloan was dispatched to meet Henry Leland, the boss of Cadillac, which had rejected a batch of the roller bearings because they did not all consistently meet the required engineering tolerance of 0.025mm.

After robustly defending his company's products, Sloan very rapidly learnt the need for consistent top quality: "*Mr Sloan, Cadillacs are made to run, not just to sell*", he was roundly told. He returned to Hyatt with clear plans for quality enhancement.

Rapid promotion

Aged just 23, he rose to become the President of the struggling Hyatt company in 1899. Under him, Hyatt roller bearings became the standard fitment across much of the automobile industry before the company was sold in 1916 as a components supplier to General Motors (GM). Here, Sloan became President of the United Motors Corporation subsidiary.

By 1918, United became an integral part of GM, with Sloan appointed to the Executive Committee. Just five years later, Sloan had risen through the ranks to become the long-serving CEO of what was to become the largest automobile manufacturer in the US (and, at one time, in the world). It was here that he made his name as an innovator of the US auto industry.

Creating structure out of chaos

GM was a sprawling conglomeration of different vehicle brands, and Sloan introduced the principle of a centralised corporate policy, together with decentralised management of the individual GM divisions. He ensured that each brand had a place in the '*ladder of success*', enabling buyers to purchase something suitable from the GM family as their spending power changed through life.

At the bottom of the ladder was entry-level Chevrolet (the largest and most successful brand), followed by mid-range Pontiac, innovative Oldsmobile, Buick (loved by the professional classes), and on to the luxurious top level of Cadillac. Creating something for all buyers prevented them from being tempted away by Ford or Chrysler. Within this hierarchy of brands, Sloan ensured that each division had autonomy and competed against each other. He was obsessed with ensuring that he appointed the best managers for the role, believing in the best fit for each position.

Sloan had become Chairman of GM in 1937, keeping the title of CEO until 1946. Upon resigning his chairmanship in 1956, the Board appointed him Honorary Chairman. This trained engineer had become an astute marketeer – recognising the pent-up demand for new models post-war.

Critics said that he was overly rational – a cold, calculating engineer devoid of other human values. He depersonalised issues, even appointing people he did not like or firing those he got on with – all in the interests of rational decisions. He was determined that trade union membership should not be an essential prerequisite for his employees. One story about his chairing a meeting illustrates much about his character. "*Gentlemen, I take it we are all in complete agreement on the decision here.*" Seeing the nods of agreement, Sloan proceeded, "*Then I propose we postpone further discussion of this matter until the next meeting to give ourselves time to develop disagreement, and perhaps gain some understanding of what the decision is about.*"

So, how to weigh up Sloan?

Sloan set the overall business vision, yet his 'flexible mass production' approach allowed autonomy, provided that quality was paramount and was attained. He introduced management practices still regarded today as enlightened. A workaholic, he had little interest in hobbies or life outside work.

He lived devotedly with his wife Irene, did not drink or smoke, and hated parties. On one occasion, he famously left Irene alone on holiday after just one day to return to work – although he was to be distraught on her later death. He formed a strong friendship with former colleague and then competitor, Walter Chrysler, who had left GM to start his own automobile company. It is rumoured that they never talked business. Likewise, where he had critics, he listened to them fully, politely and intently, asserting their right to a different point of view – even if, by the conclusion of the discussion, he rejected it.

Despite his obsession with work, he did show an interest in others, establishing the Alfred P Sloan Foundation in 1934 to provide grants for science and technology research. He also provided significant funding to the newly established Memorial Sloan-Kettering Cancer Research Center.

On the debit side, detractors point to a number of issues. His yearly re-styling of models can be viewed as the start of built-in obsolescence. When the German Opel division was taken over by the Nazi state in wartime, Sloan shrugged off accusations of supporting the Nazis, believing that it was not the job of business to get involved with politics. He reluctantly took Opel back under GM control post-war.

Sloan died in New York on February 16 1966, at the age of 90, having retained his Brooklyn drawl throughout his life. His lasting management legacy is known globally through the Sloan Management School at his alma mater, MIT. Perhaps his most telling epitaph was his self-evaluation: "*I never give orders – I sell my ideas to others if I can*".

Charles E. Sorensen: No More Mr Nice Guy

One of the most widely read self-help books of all time is Dale Carnegie's 1936 title, *How to Win Friends and Influence People.* It is unlikely to have been on the reading list of our next character, Charles Sorensen. As the introduction to this book indicates, the achievements of those characters featured may have been great, but not always their personalities.

Charles Emil Sorensen was of Danish-American heritage, born in Copenhagen but having emigrated with his parents to the US as a four-year-old in 1885. They settled in Detroit, where the young Sorensen found employment as a foundry worker at a stove works. It was here that a chance encounter with Henry Ford took place. Impressed by his passion and skills, Ford offered him a job as a pattern-maker at his new Highland Park factory.

The pattern maker translates concepts into reality

Displaying an ability to translate Ford's sketches into three-dimensional prototypes, Sorensen rose up the ranks quickly, initially as head of the pattern department in 1907. His later job titles at each of Ford's three factories were never disclosed. Henry Ford worked on a secretive basis, having a few right-hand men who could be trusted to implement his policies, but Sorensen was effectively Head of Production.

Ford nicknamed him 'Cast-Iron Charlie', partly in recognition of his stove-making past but also his unyielding demeanour. He rapidly became famous for his exceptional organisational skills, and infamous for his demanding personality and his explosive temper. Sorensen was firmly in the dictatorial management category, single-minded and not to be swayed. This suited the similarly disposed Ford, who allowed Sorensen to essentially run the River Rouge factory, introducing the Fordson tractor and modernising the Lincoln brand, recently bought from GM.

It was Sorensen who, with a small band of colleagues, envisioned the moving production line at Ford. Indeed, in his own memoir, Sorensen disputed that Henry Ford invented mass production, rather: "*He was the sponsor of it. He had nothing to do with originating, planning and carrying out the assembly line*". Sorensen was not going to let others bask in the glory of what he felt was rightfully his. In his own words:

It was then that the idea occurred to me that assembly would be easier, simpler and faster if we moved the chassis along, beginning at one end of the plant with a frame and adding the axles and the wheels; then moving it past the stockroom, instead of moving the stockroom to the chassis[8].

---

[8] Assembly Mag, https://tinyurl.com/2huhm6f4

Such 'glory' was recognised by King Christian of his native Denmark, who knighted Sorensen in 1946 as a member of the Order of Dannebrog for his accomplishments.

As Henry Ford's time at Ford began to reach its end, he appointed his son, Edsel, as his successor. Edsel could not stand Sorensen's screaming and bullying management style, so he fired him. Not for the first time, Henry overruled his son and immediately rehired Sorensen – who was to last longer at Ford than Edsel.

Skills put to good use in wartime

In the run-up to the Second World War, the US government recognised the need to expand the number of military equipment producers. 'Shadow factories' were set up, including by Ford, with Sorensen responsible for all defence contracts.

Firstly, there was Jeep, whose origin is well-known. The War Department sought bids from US companies to build a light, 4x4 'general purpose' (hence 'Jeep') utility vehicle. American Bantam and Willys-Overland submitted successful bids, but Bantam was deemed too small an operation to deliver, so it was diverted to Ford. Under Sorensen's control, Ford produced 280,448 vehicles in a rapid and consistent manner, whilst Willys produced 362,841.

More impressive still was the production by Ford of the B-24 Liberator bomber at the newly built Willow Run plant in Ypsilanti, Michigan. It was calculated that each aircraft comprised 488,193 separate parts to be assembled. The production rate was initially one per day, but – over time – Sorensen achieved the staggering production rate of one complete aircraft per hour! Exactly how did he achieve this? Two key concepts went hand in hand – break down a complex process into manageable parts; and upskill the workforce so that they can undertake a variety of assembly tasks. Sorensen divided the assembly of the aircraft into 11 major assemblies and 69 sub-assemblies. The smaller the assembly tasks, the easier it was for employees to take on multiple roles. Specialised production layouts and just-in-time delivery mechanisms contributed to speeding up the process, just as in a car factory.

Whilst Sorensen recognised that building a Ford V8 engine in comparison to a four-engine bomber was "*like comparing building a garage with a skyscraper*", the fundamental principles were the same.

'Break the design into essential units and make a separate production layout for each unit. Next, build as many units are required, then deliver each unit in its proper sequence to the assembly line to make one whole unit – a finished plane[9]*."*

During the war, Edsel Ford left the company, apparently stressed by overseeing the Willow Run factory and dealing with Sorenson's outbursts. He died young in 1943 of stomach cancer. His son, Henry Ford II, replaced him. Having been essentially the 'regent' between the rule of the two Henrys, Sorensen felt demoted by the younger Henry. He departed Ford in 1944, moving to Willys, where he was responsible for the design and production of the Jeep CJ (Civilian Jeep) post-war. Using his experience with the Jeep and Fordson tractors, he 'demilitarised' it to make it

---

[9] Sorensen C. *My Forty Years With Ford.* See bibliography.

attractive to small farmers. After clashing regularly with the Willys board, Sorensen retired fully in 1950, dying in 1968. Over the years, the Jeep brand went through a series of owners and is today part of the sprawling Stellantis conglomerate.

Sorensen's personality was unlikely to win many close colleagues. In his defence, wartime priorities brought his managerial style and vision to the fore, and the workforce rose magnificently to the challenges he set.

Freelan Oscar Stanley: His Steamer Became a Hot Number

Few entrepreneurs have had such a varied business career as Freelan Oscar Stanley – violin maker, photographic business owner, sugar refiner, hotelier and, for much of his life, manufacturer of steam-powered cars.

Born in June 1849, Freelan Oscar Stanley grew up with his twin brother, Francis Edgar, in a strict Calvinistic household in Maine, New England. Education was much-prized by his parents as the route to a righteous life. The twins started their first business, refining maple sugar, at just nine years old. By age 11, Freelan was being taught by his uncle how to make violins. This hobby continued throughout his life, and he crafted some fine instruments, including a Stradivarius-derived model for his personal use. But the twins' real interest was in things mechanical.

In the 1890s, they were running a successful dry plate photographic company in Maine, a business which made Freelan very wealthy. As a hobby, Freelan constructed a steam car in 1897. In 1898, he demonstrated its speed in front of a packed Boston grandstand, gaining not only a new world speed record but huge orders for their car. Demand soared as spectators were amazed at both its speed and its hill-climbing ability, which left petrol-engined cars way behind.

Full steam ahead for a bestseller

During 1898 and 1899, their cars became the bestselling brand in the USA, selling over two hundred vehicles. They were not powered by internal combustion engines but by steam. Full of bright marketing ideas, in August 1899, Freelan and his wife, Flora, drove one of their models to the peak of Mount Washington in New Hampshire. It was New England's highest mountain, and their journey may have inspired Henry Alexander (p124) over a decade later. It took more than two hours and was testament to the durability of the steam-car not to overheat on the steep gradient nor fall apart over the rough terrain.

Two years later, they had sold the business and the design patents of this early steam car to Locomobile. Yet, the Stanley designs were lighter and faster than their competitors, so they bought the company back, renaming it Stanley Motor Carriage Company in 1901. One of the main competitors for their photographic business had been George Eastman, the founder of Kodak, who bought them out in 1903 so that they could concentrate on building cars. Eastman was so impressed with the cars that he became one of their best customers.

Each brother focused on different aspects of the revitalised business – Francis on manufacturing and Freelan on marketing. Freelan dreamed up the slogan that petrol-engined cars caused "*fear, uncertainty and doubt*", playing on public concerns that an internal combustion engine might explode. Stanley steam-cars were famous for their quiet and smooth operation. Speed, too, was a sales feature of the cars, and in 1906,

Freelan set a speed record of 127 mph, phenomenal for its time and not broken for another four years.

Over time, the appearance and design of the cars changed. Early cars featured a rear boiler, but from 1905-1915, they adopted a more modern appearance, sporting what owners nicknamed a 'coffin-nosed' front boiler. From 1915-1924, they had a yet more conventional appearance, in line with their petrol competitors. Despite these updates, sales dwindled, particularly from 1912 with the introduction of the electric starter motor (see Charles Kettering p88), which made a petrol-engined car so much easier to run. A contributing factor was also cost – by 1924, a Stanley 740D cost virtually $4,000, whilst a Model T Ford was just $500.

Illness sparks a new interest

In 1903, Freelan was again struck down by tuberculosis, which he had first suffered in 1881. He sought a variety of treatments, including from Dr Charles Bonney, the nation's leading authority on the condition. Bonney advised recuperating in the pure mountain air of Colorado, particularly Estes Park, which had a similar climate to the Swiss tuberculosis resort of Davos.

Freelan set off by car that June and, by the end of the summer in Estes Park, his health had improved noticeably. So much so, that for the next four years, he travelled every summer to a nearby rented property. In 1907, he decided to build a prestigious hotel there, the Stanley Hotel, for wealthy city dwellers similarly afflicted with the condition. As with everything Freelan did, he entered into the task fully, enthusiastically and with the aim of achieving the highest quality. He built a hydro-electric plant to supply electricity to the area, a laundry (steam, naturally), a lift, telephones and 48 well-appointed guest bedrooms. A keen music lover, Freelan ensured that the concert hall hosted a Steinway piano. A range of outdoor activities was available to guests, together with formal and informal evening entertainment. Not surprisingly, Stanley Steamers provided a shuttle service to and from the hotel!

Environmental focus

During his life, Freelan's dedication to the natural environment was instrumental in establishing the Rocky Mountain National Park. This area was now his summertime home, and by 1917, he was gradually transferring his interest from the steam car company to the hotel, sanatoria, and to philanthropy. He endowed a high school in his native Kingfield, Maine. That year, both he and Francis stepped down from managing the car company. With tragic irony, Francis, whilst driving a Stanley Steamer, was killed in a car accident in 1918. Despite total sales of around 14,000 cars, Freelan could see that the end of his beloved steam cars was nigh. The factory and business closed in 1924.

Long after his involvement with steam cars, Freelan paid a visit in 1933 to Henry Ford, now dominating the automobile business. Ford decided to buy several of his models – not cars but violins, which Freelan had lovingly crafted over the years. Indeed, it is said that Freelan's 'happy place' was his violin workshop.

Flora, his beloved wife, suffered from deteriorating eyesight and died after a stroke in 1939. A lifelong teetotaller and non-smoker, Freelan died of heart failure the following year.

The hotel finds new fame

But that was not the end of the story of his Stanley Hotel, which continued under new ownership. On 30 October 1974, a Mr and Mrs Stephen King visited the hotel to find that they were the last guests in a deserted hotel before the annual scheduled winter closure. As he explored the eerie hotel corridors alone, Mr King entered a bathroom and the thought struck him: "*What if someone died here? At that moment, I knew I had a book.*" And so '*The Shining*' was born.

What continues to 'shine' are the surviving Stanley Steamer cars, lovingly maintained and displayed by a passionate band of devotees. Keep a lookout for one at a summer car festival.

A Stanley Steamer

Preston Tucker: The Little Guy Who Took On The Major Corporations

Take a look at any Hollywood film of the late 1940s, and the cars featured don't look very different from their pre-war counterparts. Little engineering progress was evident; they still had a 1930s appearance with separate front mudguards and steeply raked windscreens. You get the picture. Of course, post-war, the big three auto manufacturers (Ford, Chrysler and General Motors) were reverting to car production after years of reliably churning out military vehicles and planes on government instruction. Raw materials, particularly steel, were in short supply, yet manufacturers were encouraged to produce cars quickly to satisfy public demand. There was little scope for new designs.

A master of innovation

Preston Tucker thought otherwise. His life had been focused on cars, selling multiple brands and even joining the local police department several times because he wanted to drive their patrol cars … until he was sacked for blow-torching a hole in the dashboard to allow the engine heat to warm the passenger compartment on wintry shifts.

Tucker had previously designed an armoured personnel vehicle (turned down by the US military because, able to exceed 100mph, it was too fast to use in combat situations). Undeterred, he designed a revolving aircraft turret dome – the Tucker Turret – to enhance the gunner's aiming precision. The military liked this innovation and Tucker started its production in the shed next to his house in Ypsilanti, Michigan, under the name Ypsilanti Machine and Tool Company. This city was also the home of the Willow Run factory building the B-24 Liberator aircraft (see Charles Sorenson), although that used a competing dome, the Sperry. Indeed, ultimately, no aircraft manufacturer except Douglas was to adopt Tucker's design.

Post-war, his vision for the new Tucker 48 car was as maverick as his personality. Safety features, elegant design and advanced engineering were well ahead of the competition. The long list of features included: a rear engine, a third directional headlight which swivelled, an integral roll bar in the roof, lap seat belts, a locking parking brake to deter theft, collapsible steering column, doors which extended into the roofline to ease entry and exit, a safety-glass windscreen which popped out on impact, a padded dashboard, radio as standard and very aerodynamic lines. Some individual ideas were from donor cars – after all, the original model contained scrapyard components.

A 1948 Tucker Torpedo

Boundless enthusiasm

Next, Tucker wanted to buy the largest factory in the world, and to demonstrate that he could meet orders, he even started selling accessories for the as-yet unbuilt cars. That way, he could 'demonstrate' the vehicle sales he had lined up, and existing car dealers were signed up as Tucker dealers. All these ploys demonstrated Tucker's unbreakable optimism, enthusiasm and ability to convince financial backers and the public alike. The chain-smoking entrepreneur bounced from problem to problem, with the energetic and enthusiastic support of his family and a small team of engineers.

Not surprisingly, the big three automobile manufacturers wanted to strangle this upstart at birth. They alone had the mass production know-how, the contacts with component suppliers, and the access to traditional markets. They also traded on the perception that they had done their bit for the war effort in producing the stalwart GM and Studebaker military trucks and the Jeep. This complacency and hesitancy extended to Tucker's own board of directors. They lacked vision and courage and were keen to revert to conventional designs.

Indeed, Tucker encountered considerable problems with his prototype. Changes to the original design purity had to be made to engine choice, transmission and suspension. Without the skills of designer Alex Tremulis, in making Tucker's vision workable, the Tucker 48 would never have made it to production.

Financial and legal hurdles kill the innovative car

Tucker found that steel cost him three times as much as the big corporations paid their suppliers. Furthermore, he had upset the Securities and Exchange Commission (SEC), who suspected fraud on a large scale. (Tucker's supporters claimed that the SEC engineered bogus fraud.) The SEC claimed that the cars did not exist, the factory – far away from his competitors' territory – was non-existent, and that the company's financial dealings were fraudulent. After a lengthy and bitter court battle, Tucker was found innocent of the charges and generated considerable public goodwill for his aspirational, inspirational and creative thinking.

But it was too late to save the company and the car. The delays, bad press and loss of investors brought an end to the dream of an innovative car for Americans. Undeterred, the serial entrepreneur bounced on to his next challenge – the Carioca sports car to be built in Brazil. But within a few years, ill-health had overtaken this heavy smoker, and he died of pneumonia as a complication of lung cancer at the early age of 53 on Boxing Day 1956.

This trailblazing car was featured in the 1988 film *Tucker: The Man and His Dream*, directed by Francis Ford Coppola. A strange choice of project for such a renowned director? Not when you know that he is the proud owner of a Tucker, displayed in his vineyard. As the film's closing credits reveal, of the 51 cars produced in double-quick time, an astounding 47 of them were still in fine working order at the time of filming.

Felix Wankel: Rotor Motor Man

The development of the four-cycle internal combustion engine has seen many changes over the years by engineers and designers pushing the boundaries of performance, reliability and efficiency. The designs all adopt the four-cycles of traditional engines – intake, compression, expansion and exhaust. We have had inline engines, transverse engines, V-layouts, and 'boxer' engines.

Variations on engineering principles have included two-stroke engines (Trabants and early Saabs) and, of course, heavier engines powered by diesel fuel. They all have cylinders pounding in a specific sequence within a large engine block. Step forward Felix Wankel, and his revolutionary design of a rotary engine. Instead of multiple pistons powering away inside a cylinder block, Wankel was absorbed from an early age with finding an alternative approach.

The self-taught engineer

Born in 1902, Felix grew up in Swabia, southern Germany in the early part of the twentieth century. His forestry worker father was called up to fight in the First World War and was killed in action when Felix was just 12. This left his family in straitened circumstances, and Felix was unable to attend university to train as an engineer. Nevertheless, he became obsessed with making the concept of the rotary engine work; whilst it was established as a concept, no one had succeeded in building a reliable one. So, he became a self-educated engineer, opening a small repair shop in Heidelberg.

It was the 1930s, a time of privation when many people, including Felix, went hungry. Who could offer the answers to this poverty? As well as his attraction to the rotary principle, Felix was also attracted by the political principles of the Nazis, who seemed to offer an answer to the economic and social problems of the country. He joined several anti-Semitic groups, leading youth groups and undertaking leading paramilitary training and scouting. It was his focus on military training – as opposed to political ends – which saw him expelled from the Nazis in 1932, even being arrested and imprisoned for six months. By wartime in 1940, however, he had become an Obersturmbannführer in the SS. He was unable to become a combatant because of his dreadful eyesight.

Wartime experimentation

Wankel continued working in the Lake Constance region, home to several aeronautical companies (such as Dornier and Zeppelin). He worked on developing seals, rotary valves and experimental rotary engines for aircraft and automobile manufacturers, and was determined to design an engine which was lighter and more powerful than conventional piston engines.

In his workshop, he developed a stationary rotary engine with a unique gasket – the gasket having been a problem for previous experiments with the rotary principle. At the end of the war, in common with many other manufacturers, his workshop was dismantled by the Allies, who feared rearmament of German industry.

All his working notes were confiscated, and he was imprisoned, this time as a prisoner of war.

Success with NSU and Mazda

Post-war, Wankel was able to resume his engineering work, gaining work with the Neckarsulm Strickmaschinen Union. It was a former knitting machine company which had diversified into vehicle manufacture as NSU Motorenwerk AG. It built small motorcycles and mopeds with some success. (In later years, the Quickly moped was to be popular in the UK, together with the Prinz budget cars.) Wankel completed his first design of a rotary engine for NSU in 1954, exhibiting his thoroughly-researched prototype in 1956. Forming his own company, Wankel GmbH, he licensed the design in return for royalties.

Instead of pistons furiously powering cylinders, a rotary engine has a triangular rotor orbiting inside a sealed, static chamber. Each rotation allows the four elements of the cycle to be completed in a more compact layout. The perceived advantages are lighter weight, fewer parts, smaller size and smoothness. Over the years, two manufacturers have become synonymous with the rotary engine – NSU and the Japanese company Mazda. The NSU Ro80 was a twin-rotor, high-tech luxury saloon which gained the Car of the Year award in 1968. It looked sleek then and still looks modern all these years on. In total, NSU produced 40,000 rotor-powered cars across several models.

An NSU Ro 80

The Mazda RX8 sports car (produced till 2012) was able to produce an astonishing 255bhp from a 1.3 litre engine. Its Renesis engine won the 2003 International Engine of the Year award and weighed only 112kg, substantially lighter than a traditional engine.

A Wankel Rotary Engine from a Mazda RX-7

At the time of writing, Mazda uses a tiny rotary engine in its MX30 car, but it does not drive the car directly; it powers the battery.

An incomplete success?

Success allowed Felix to gradually leave poverty behind, although full engineering recognition was to come only after his death. So, why has the rotary engine not become more widely adopted? Maybe because it is just too different. Or is it the wear of the rotor tips requiring periodic repair, or the potentially greater fuel consumption because of inferior thermodynamic properties of the engine block? Nevertheless, engineers have seen potential in the design for hydrogen engines, so we have not seen the last of the rotary engine.

Felix's poor eyesight meant that he never held a driving licence himself but was to be seen being chauffeured around in an NSU Ro80 in the 1970s. Shortly before his death in 1988, he sold his Felix Wankel Institute to Daimler-Benz for a reported 100 million Deutsche Marks. For someone who never attended university, he was granted several honorary doctorates, including in 1969 from the prestigious Munich Technical University, a fellow alumnus of which had been Rudolf Diesel.

It remains the case that this imaginative and industrious engineer never found the recognition he deserved during his lifetime.

Margaret Wilcox: Transforming Vehicle Comfort

Search online for any female automotive invention pioneer and the name Margaret Wilcox will pop up. You may feel, at first, that her invention was tangential to motoring, but as we shall see, its adaptation is now integral to all vehicles, enhancing vehicle safety.

If you have already read about Mary Anderson (p3), you will know of the struggles that female designers and inventors encountered in the early twentieth-century USA. Margaret Wilcox was born in Chicago in 1838, and little is known about her early life because it was common then for women's roles and histories to be overshadowed by men's. But we do know that she demonstrated an interest in, and aptitude for, engineering from an early age. Against the odds, her vision, determination and persistence led to an invention we now all take for granted.

Chicago was a bustling, rapidly expanding northern city close to the Great Lakes. It was the centre of the US meat industry, and its cattle stockyards and meat production facilities were enormous. The meat and cattle industries led to the city becoming the railroad hub of the US, spawning also the huge catalogue mail-order operations of Sears Roebuck, which sent parcels nationwide. The local Chicago City Railway also provided well-used rapid transport around what was nicknamed the 'windy city'. As a result, railroad cars were familiar to Chicago residents who used them extensively and were vital to the rapidly growing economy.

It was aboard such a railway 'car' that Margaret Wilcox got her original idea. Chicago, being so close to the Canadian border, is notoriously cold in the winter. As there was no railcar heating, passengers would often actually feel colder sitting on the train than if they were walking outside, where they could benefit from the warmth brought about by exercise. Yet steam engines themselves obviously generate a lot of heat. How, Margaret wondered, could some of the heat created by the locomotive be channelled into the passenger coaches to keep the passengers warmer?

The heat is on

Margaret set about designing a system to solve the problem. For most of the nineteenth century, women in the USA were not allowed to submit a patent in their own name, only in their father's or husband's name. Margaret knew this as she had invented appliances earlier in her life (for example, a combination washing machine and dishwasher). For this invention, she had been required to submit the patent in her husband's name but – unfortunately – Margaret had lost her husband in 1883, so now had to fend for herself in life, including her inventions. In 1893, the world's Columbian Exposition (also known as the Chicago World's Fair) came to her home city, and she took the opportunity to present her train carriage heater concept there. Fortunately for Margaret, the patent law had changed earlier that year, so she had been able to submit legitimately in her own name and been granted a patent.

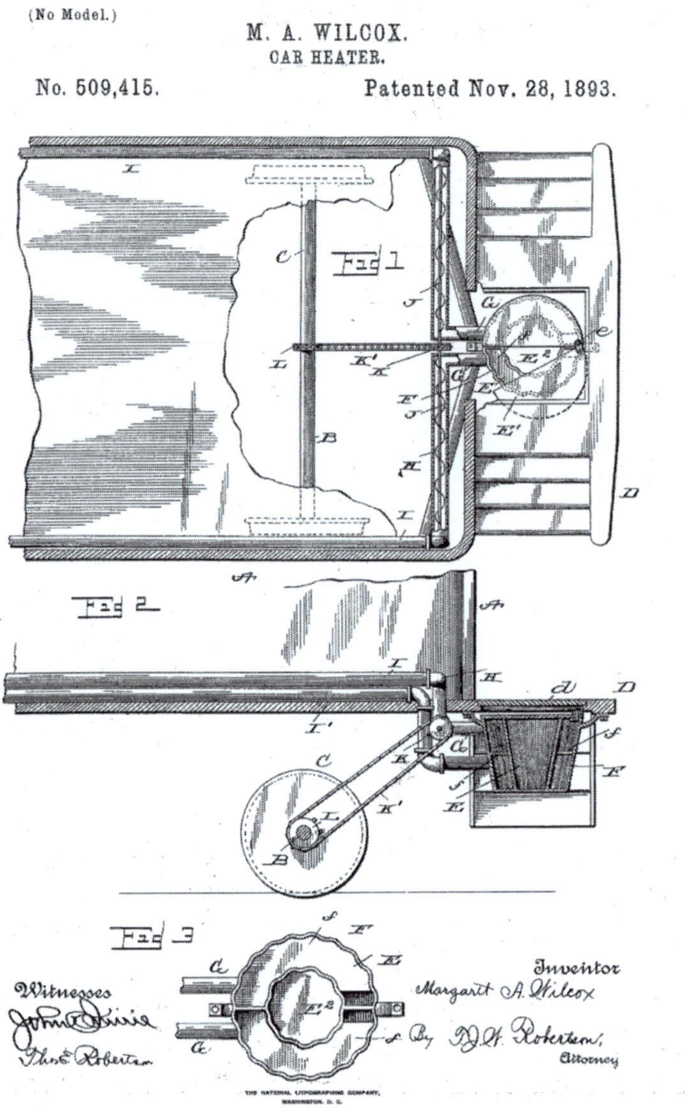

It was a fairly basic design, running a channel of air from the engine heat source into the passenger compartment, warming the compartment and demisting the windows. This simple, ingenious idea had a snag, though. There was no way to regulate the temperature either up or down. The heater simply emitted heat with no user control, whether by passengers or the train manager. The longer the journey, the hotter it got, cooling only when the train was stationary. The unfortunate choice for passengers was either to be cold without the heater or too hot with it on. Hardly ideal. But, to her credit, nobody had thought of the idea before, so let's not be critical.

Over time, the concept would prove attractive to automobile manufacturers. Looking back at the early days of motoring, it is difficult to understand why such an idea to transform the comfort of driver and passengers could be so overlooked. However, in reality, early motor cars had been open-topped and mostly used in fine weather (as Mary Anderson found out with manufacturers' reluctance to adopt windscreen wipers). We're so used to seeing images of that era featuring passengers well wrapped-up against the elements, even in summer conditions, that we can forget the lack of other wind-cheating protection or devices. From 1907, enclosed passenger compartments for some cars were introduced, allowing all-weather use, and the first rudimentary car heaters were used from 1917 – alas, five years after Margaret's death in Los Angeles in 1912.

In the same way that, for example, modern vehicle tyres have developed significantly from John Boyd Dunlop's original pneumatic concept, so too has Margaret Wilcox's initial concept progressed through considerable development and refinement to become the sophisticated climate-control systems we now see in many vehicles.

Adapted for cars

The real breakthrough for car heating came in 1929 when Ford started to install heaters in their Model A cars – although many manufacturers offered them only as an optional extra for many more decades. Even in the 1960s, heaters were often considered an optional luxury, particularly for fleet specification vehicles. Take a look at the entry on Preston Tucker (p176) to see how he adapted his work car in the 1930s to allow heat into the passenger compartment!

These days, we take it for granted that we can easily adjust the inside temperature of a vehicle to suit us, whatever the weather outside. And that applies to cars, trains and aircraft. For that, we have to thank Margaret. In 2020, Margaret's heater patent was named by Inventor's Digest as one of the top ten patents by women. It was also a recognition that good ideas were not restricted to originating from college-educated males – but also an intuitively-designed concept from someone who felt strongly that passenger travel could be more bearable.

Women Workers at Fords of Dagenham: "*We want sex...*"

You can't sell a car with no seats. That's what Ford of Britain found out in 1968 when every sewing machinist at their Dagenham plant went on strike. They were responsible for crafting and assembling the fabric onto the seat frames for all cars and vans produced at Ford's largest UK site.

Whilst their strike was to prove disruptive for Ford, it created a huge social history and industrial relations legacy, and brought about the introduction of the UK's 1970 Equal Pay Act.

Downgrading of skills

But why were the 187 women on strike when the men assembling the cars on the production line were still at work? Ford had recently downgraded their work from Grade C – skilled labour – to Grade B – unskilled labour. Yet men doing a similar job (e.g., leather cutters and spray painters) in the plant were still graded as skilled. It was not just the terminology. Skilled workers earned 15% more than unskilled ones. The women wanted equal pay with men, not just for doing the same job, but for doing work they deemed to be of equal value. These were ordinary working class women from the East End of London, but their determination, tenacity and sense of a just cause would contribute to a change in employment legislation for the whole nation.

On 7 June 1968, a strike was called, supported by the majority of the workers, although shop steward, Lil O'Callaghan, had to persuade the male union convenor to support their action. Not all the workers were happy about the strike. A significant number of men regarded the women as working for only 'pin money' and whose action was putting their own livelihoods and the future of the plant at risk.

Letter to Prime Minister

The women, led by Rose Boland and 'Effing' Eileen Pullen (noted for her colourful language), were deadly serious about their cause. So much so that they wrote a collective letter signed by the 'women workers at Fords of Dagenham' to the Prime Minister, Harold Wilson. It is transcribed verbatim below from the original in the National Archives:

Women Workers of Fords

June 1968

Dear Mr Wilson,

You can call all the enquiries you wish we women at fords have the backing of a great number of M.P's, we will not go back to work, we are fighting a great fight equal pay for women, we at Fords have started the ball rolling our unions are backing us, funds are coming in we're all set for battle, Fords is the beginning, soon it will be every industry in Britain out because of us women of Fords, we will force you to give us all equal pay, or strike with our unions blessings, we're sorry for Fords, sorry for the men out of work but more sorry for ourselves its all for us now. Some women may be hard up we'll help them from our growing funds, make no mistake most of us have husbands still working thats why we can fight you all, we are only our own money short, we will live. Give us what we want, not only us at Fords all Women everywhere, we refuse to go back, so what can you and the government & Mrs Castle & Jack Scamp do. Nothing I mean nothing, we are sitting pretty our unions are backing us. Show this to Barbara, we don't care M.P's are with us, soon everyone will be with us we will make Fords shut down completely, who cares we dont.

Women Workers at Fords of Dagenham.

Give us what our unions demand equal pay.

On 28 June 1968, the women boarded a coach and headed off to London, where they paraded in Whitehall with their banners. "*We want sex …*" read one, which had not yet been fully unfurled to read the final word "*equality*". That was enough for some press photographers and newspapers, for whom that banner became a trivialised headline about the industrial struggle. According to a 2013 interview with the *Guardian* on the 45th anniversary of the Whitehall demonstration, Gwen Davis, by now an 80-year-old, laughingly blamed her fellow machinist, Vera Sime, for the mishap.

But matters got serious. It was the first time that female workers at Ford had forced a stoppage, bringing all car and van production to a complete halt. Ford predicted at the outbreak of the strike that, within a week, 3,000 to 5,000 men could be laid off and the plant permanently damaged. As reported in the *Barking & Dagenham Post*, a spokesperson for the shop stewards' committee said:

"This is as indefensible as colour and race issues. The girls feel that they have a trade. This is discrimination entirely on sex grounds."

The women remained determined, with one reported in the *Post* on 12 June as saying: "*We know what we want – we won't give up until we get it*".

Tea at Downing Street

Ford was determined not to respond to their demands. After six weeks of strike action, it took the government's Secretary of State for Employment, Barbara Castle, to become involved. She invited Rose and her union colleagues to a meeting in Downing Street. No male union or company representatives were allowed, just women. As a result, Ford accepted increasing the women's pay to 92% of the men's rate, and an inquiry was set up to look at re-grading and equal funding. However, the inquiry did not support the women's case.

Machinists' legacy

The women were only re-graded to full equality after a further seven-week strike in 1984. Yet, their 92% victory was the inspiration for several fictional adaptations of the dispute – the 2010 film *Made in Dagenham* and its musical spin-off. Both these productions brought the women's struggle to a wider audience, ensuring that many more people learnt of the enduring impact the women made on British social, industrial and motoring history. As former Barking MP, now Baroness, Margaret Hodge, declared: "*Dagenham women really made history*".

Their legacy lives on in some of the street names of the new Dagenham Green residential development on the site of the demolished factory. Additionally, in February 2018, Rose Boland was one of 13 shortlisted nominees for BBC Radio 4's *Today* programme's poll of 'the most influential women', alongside suffragettes, scientists and Queen Elizabeth II.

Women Workers from the Ford Motor Company plant in Dagenham

Select Bibliography

By their very nature, little-known motoring heroes have few books written about them – something this book is attempting to change. Other sources of information, notably Wikipedia, will have information about some. For US innovators, the website https://www.automotivehalloffame.org/ features those who have been inducted into their Hall of Fame.

There are dedicated websites which contain some useful information (www.mercedes-benz.com, below, about Bertha Benz, for example) or regional newspapers about some entrants (e.g., Yorkshire newspapers on Percy Shaw or Ivan Hirst). I have written articles about some characters in *Good Motoring* magazine and the journal of the *Road Transport History Association* (entries below). Note that the archive of Road Transport History Association articles is freely available at: https://rchs.org.uk/road-transport-history-association-archive/

Likewise, some specialist automobile-related publishers have beautifully produced and expensive books on some heroes (a few are listed below).

However, here are some additional sources which you may find online or in your local library.

Henry Alexander Jr.

https://www.bbc.co.uk/news/uk-scotland-highlands-islands-44003271

https://player.bfi.org.uk/free/film/watch-motoring-over-ben-nevis-1911-online

Mary Anderson

Ashley, R. A True Star of Screen … and an unsung hero of Motoring *Good Motoring* Winter 2023. p60-61

Bertha Benz

https://www.mercedes-benz.com/en/innovation/milestones/gallery-of-legends/

Nils Bohlin

See entry at https://www.history.com/this-day-in-history/july-17/three-point-seatbelt-inventor-nils-bohlin-born

Violette Cordery

http://intriguing-people.com/author/imogen/

Tony Crook

https://www.goodwood.com/grr/f1/tony-crook-the-man-who-kept-bristol-cars-alive--thank-frankel-its-friday/

William Knox D'Arcy

Koram, K. (2022). *Uncommon Wealth: Britain and the Aftermath of Empire*. London: John Murray Press.

Rudolf Diesel

Ashley, R. The Surprising Story of Rudolf Diesel: His Life and Achievements Re-examined. The Road Transport History Association. *Journal* 109. Oct 2022, 1-7.

W. Robert Nitske & Charles Morrow Wilson. (1965). *Rudolf Diesel: Pioneer of the Age of Power*. Norman: University of Oklahoma Press.

John Boyd Dunlop

Cooke, J. (2015). *John Boyd Dunlop*. Dreoilin: Carristown, Co. Meath.

Gilbern

Burgess, M. (2019). *Gilbern Cars*. Stroud: Amberley.

Alma Green

Martinez, V. (2019). https://abitofhistoryblog.com/2019/03/25/the-mother-of-the-green-book-ignored-by-history/

Donald Healey

Healey, D. (1989). *My World of Cars*. Cambridge: Patrick Stephens.

John D. Hertz

Alef, D. (2009). *John D Hertz: Patron of Taxis and Buses.* Titans of Fortune Publishing e-book.

https://www.hertzfoundation.org/about-us/our-history/

Ivan Hirst

Ashley, R. The Soldier Who Saved Volkswagen. *Good Motoring* Autumn 2024 p56-57

https://www.keymilitary.com/article/major-intervention

Soichiro Honda

Hazlewood, M. (2023). *The Poor Boy Who Created Honda.* Business Success Stories via Amazon.

Leslie Hore Belisha

Grimwood, I. R. (2006). *A Little Chit of a Fellow: Biography of the Right Hon. Leslie Hore-Belisha.* Market Harborough: Book Guild Publishing.

https://www.jewsfww.uk/leslie-hore-belisha-mp.php

Leslie Hounsfield

https://insidecroydon.com/2025/02/16/from-brooke-bond-vans-to-bubblecars-trojan-was-in-top-gear/

Rance, E & Williams, D. (1999). *Can You Afford To Walk? The History of the Hounsfield Trojan Motor Car.* Witney: Bookmarque Publishing.

Mercedes Jellinek

Ashley, R. Little-known Motoring Heroes: pioneers you may never have heard of. The Road Transport History Association. *Journal* no. 87. Feb 2017. p 21-23

Camille Jenatzy

https://www.jenatzy.com/index.php?The+Jenatzy+Story

Charles Kettering

Boyd, Thomas Alvin. (2002). *Charles F Kettering: A Biography.* Maryland: Beard Books.

Derrenberger, R. G. https://kb.osu.edu/server/api/core/bitstreams/71e809ed-2945-5b46-9a57-cdedbbbe0422/content

Frederick Lanchester

https://lanchesterinteractive.org/ (Devised by Coventry University, which was previously known as Lanchester Polytechnic.)

Dorothy Levitt

Levitt, D. E. (1909). *The Woman and the Car: A Chatty Little Handbook for all Women Who Motor or Want To Motor.* London: John Lane.

Barton, M. W. (2022). *Fast Lady – The Extraordinary Adventures of Miss Dorothy Levitt.* Preston: Butterfield Press.

Peter Lunati

Various documents online.

https://www.tkelevator.com/us-en/company/insights/hydraulic-heritage.html

Graves of WW1 Veterans: Facebook.

https://www.facebook.com/groups/WWIVeterans/posts/1346572406059146/

Bruce McLaren

McLaren, B. (1964). *From The Cockpit.* Sherborne: Evro. (autobiography)

https://www.mclaren.com/racing/team/be-brave-beginning-3175496/

Garrett A. Morgan

Oluonye, M. N. (2008). *Garrett Augustus Morgan – Businessman, Inventor, Good Citizen.* Bloomington, Indiana: Author House.

Pat Moss Carlsson

Carlsson, E. & Moss, P. (1965). *The Art & Technique of Driving.* London: Heinemann.

Turner, S. (2011). *Harnessing Horsepower: The Pat Moss Carlsson Story.* Dorchester: Veloce.

Alex Moulton

Alex Moulton: From Bristol to Bradford upon Avon – a lifetime in engineering. (2009). Derby: The Rolls-Royce Heritage Trust.

Ransom E. Olds

Niemeyer, G. A. (1963). *The Automotive Career of Ransom E Olds.* East Lansing: University of Michigan.

Gerald Palmer

Balfour, Christopher (1998). *Auto-Architect: The Autobiography of Gerald Palmer.* London: Magna Press.

Armand Peugeot

Casucci, P. (1988). *Armand Peugeot.* Milan: Automobilia. (multi-lingual)

Dorothée Pullinger

https://www.themotormuseuminminiature.co.uk/inv-doroth%C3%A9e-pullinger.php

https://www.garnockconnections.org.uk/news/206-pullinger

William Rootes

Carverhill, G. (2018). *The Rootes Story: The Making of a Global Automotive Empire.* Ramsbury: Crowood.

Percy Shaw

Ashley, R. Little-known Motoring Heroes: pioneers you may never have heard of. The Road Transport History Association. *Journal* no. 87. Feb 2017. p 21-23.

https://museums.calderdale.gov.uk/percy-shaw

Alfred P. Sloan

Alfred P. Sloan. (1963). *My Years With General Motors.* Simon & Schuster (and various reprints by other publishers.)

Charles E. Sorensen.

Charles E. Sorensen. (1956). *My Forty Years With Ford.* New York: Norton.

https://www.assemblymag.com/articles/82847-assembly-then-now-the-man-behind-the-moving-assembly-line

Preston Tucker

Lehto, S. (2016). *Preston Tucker and his Battle to Build the Car of Tomorrow.* Chicago: Chicago Review Press.

Linde, Arvid. (2011). *Preston Tucker and others: Tales of brilliant innovators and innovations.* Dorchester: Veloce.

Felix Wankel

Faith, N. (1976). *The Wankel Engine – The Story of the Revolutionary Rotary Engine.* London: George Allen & Unwin.

Margaret Wilcox

https://www.jalopnik.com/meet-margaret-wilcox-the-woman-who-invented-the-car-he-1846657270/

Women Workers of Ford Dagenham

Collective letter to Prime Minister, Harold Wilson: Made in Dagenham: Archives Uncovered. *National Archives*:

https://www.nationalarchives.gov.uk/explore-the-collection/stories/letter-by-the-women-workers-at-fords-of-dagenham/

Extracts from *Barking & Dagenham Post*:

https://www.barkinganddagenhampost.co.uk/lifestyle/20918831.im-glad-it-ford-dagenham-workers-recall-strikes/

https://www.theguardian.com/politics/2013/jun/06/dagenham-sewing-machinists-strike

Image Credits

Mary Anderson: both images Wikimedia | **Bertha Benz:** Wikimedia | **Nils Bohlin:** Classic Picture Library/Alamy stock photo | **Violet Cordery:** Wikimedia | **Tony Crook:** GPL-Fred Taylor/Alamy stock photo | **William Knox Darcy:** public domain/Alamy stock photo | **Rudolf Diesel:** Wikimedia | **John Boyd Dunlop:** Wikimedia | **Gilbern:** Wikimedia | **Alma Green:** both images Wikimedia | **Donald Healey:** National Motor Museum/Alamy stock photo | **Red Austin-Healey 100:** Wikimedia | **John D Hertz:** FLHC DBAP1/Alamy stock photo | **Ivan Hirst:** Sueddeutsche Zeitung Photo/Alamy stock photo | **Soichiro Honda:** YG-Sport-Photos/Alamy stock photo | **Leslie Hore-Belisha:** Lebrecht Music & Arts/Alamy stock photo | **Leslie Hounsfield:** Grace's Guide | **Leyland Trojan:** Wikimedia | **Mercédès Adrienne Ramona Manuela Jellinek:** Wikimedia | **Camille Jenatzy:** Wikimedia | **Charles F Kettering:** Wikimedia | **Frederick W Lanchester:** Wikimedia | **Dorothy Levitt:** Heritage Image Partnership Ltd/Alamy stock photo | **Rotary Lift:** courtesy of Vehicle Service Group | **Bruce McLaren:** Heritage Image Partnership Ltd/Alamy stock photo | **Garrett Morgan:** IanDagnall Computing/Alamy stock photo | **Pat Moss Carlsson:** Wikimedia | **Alex Moulton:** Trinity Mirror/Mirrorpix/Alamy stock photo | **Henry Alexander:** Wikimedia | **Ransom E. Olds:** Wikimedia | **Oldsmobile Curved Dash:** Heritage Image Partnership Ltd/Alamy stock photo | **Gerald Palmer:** Wikimedia | **Jowett Javelin:** Dale Drinnon/Alamy stock photo | **Peugeot Grinder:** Rod Ashley | **Armand Peugeot:** Wikimedia | **Galloway 10.20:** Wikimedia | **Billy Rootes:** Wikimedia | **Rootes Building:** Wikimedia | **Percy Shaw:** PA Images/Alamy stock photo | **Alfred P. Sloan:** Everett Collection Inc/Alamy stock photo | **Charles E. Sorensen:** From the collections of The Henry Ford, Dearborn, Michigan | **Freelan Oscar Stanley:** Wikimedia | **Stanley Steamer:** Wikimedia | **Preston Tucker:** Wikimedia | **Tucker Torpedo:** Wikimedia | **Felix Wankel:** Wikimedia | **NSU Ro 80:** Wikimedia | **Wankel Rotary Engine from a Mazda RX-7:** Wikimedia | **Margaret Wilcox heater design:** Wikimedia | **Women Workers at Ford of Dagenham:** Trinity Mirror/Mirrorpix/Alamy stock photo

Another Book from Rod Ashley

Wolfram Wars: Exposing The Secret Battle in Portugal

Wolfram – also known as Tungsten – is about more than electric light bulbs. Its more deadly claim-to-fame rests in its armour-piercing qualities.

During WWII, Wolfram was in great demand with both the Allies and Axis powers who scoured the globe for the precious material; indeed, they deployed huge resources to secure supplies whilst simultaneously doing their best to sabotage and undermine one another.

The greatest beneficiary from these shadowy dealings was Portugal, a neutral country, under the control of the mercurial António de Oliveira Salazar. The sudden surge in demand created great wealth and bustling 'gold rush towns' deep in Portugal's remote mountainous interior, but threatened to undermine Salazar's grand vision for his country.

Wolfram Wars examines the role of Portugal in the Wolfram trade, alongside the exploits of its British, American and German customers. It takes in the glitz and glamour of wartime Lisbon, the mischievous dealings of intelligence services, and includes some of WWII's most interesting spies – spies with code names such as Garbo, Tricycle, and Treasure. A certain young intelligence officer and creator of James Bond – Ian Fleming – also has a role to play.

Appealing to connoisseurs of WWII history, *Wolfram Wars* is a story that offers adventure, intrigue and espionage, and a fascinating insight into this little-known but hugely important aspect to the war.